Wonders

Mc Graw Hill Education

Cover and Title Pages: Nathan Love

www.mheonline.com/readingwonders

Send all inquiries to:
McGraw-Hill Education
Two Penn Plaza
New York, NY 10121

ISBN: 978-0-02-134098-9
MHID: 0-02-134098-6

Printed in the United States of America.

7 8 9 LWI 21 20   E

Wonders

Program Authors

Diane August

Donald R. Bear

Janice A. Dole

Jana Echevarria

Douglas Fisher

David Francis

Vicki Gibson

Jan Hasbrouck

Margaret Kilgo

Jay McTighe

Scott G. Paris

Timothy Shanahan

Josefina V. Tinajero

Mc
Graw
Hill
Education

4

Go Digital! http://connected.mcgraw-hill.com

THE BIG IDEA

Animal Discoveries

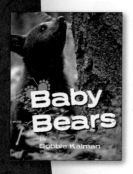

Lee Cates/Photodisc/Getty Images

Go Digital! http://connected.mcgraw-hill.com

UNIT 3

THE BIG IDEA

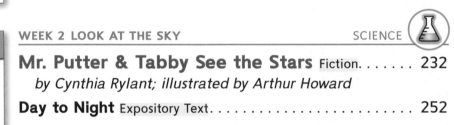
Live and Learn

Go Digital! http://connected.mcgraw-hill.com

UNIT 4

Our Life/Our World

Go Digital! http://connected.mcgraw-hill.com

Sverrir Thorolfsson Iceland/Flickr/Getty Images

THE BIG IDEA

Let's Make a Difference

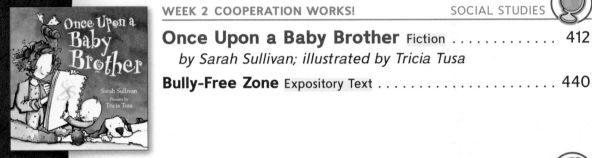
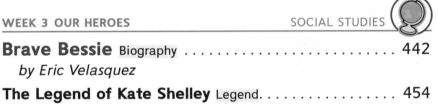
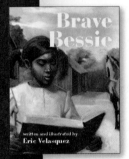

Go Digital! http://connected.mcgraw-hill.com

HELP!

A Story of Friendship

By

Holly Keller

Essential Question

How do friends depend on each other?

Read about animal friends who help each other out.

Go Digital!

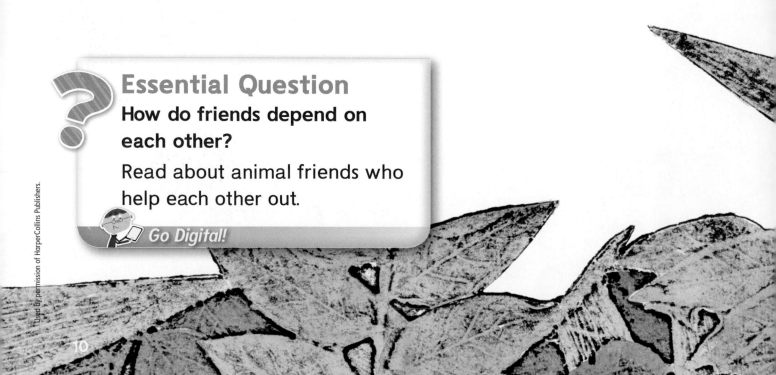

One morning Hedgehog found Mouse covering himself with leaves.

"What in the world are you doing?" asked Hedgehog.

"I'm hiding," said Mouse, "from Snake."

"From our *friend* Snake?" asked Hedgehog.

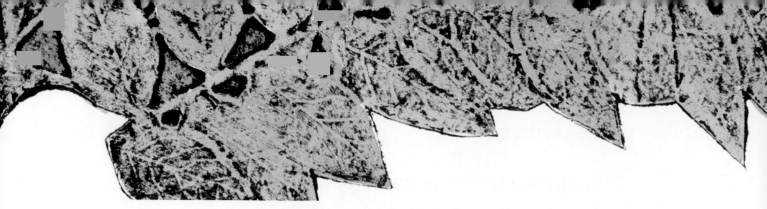

"Yes," Mouse whispered. "Fox told Skunk and Skunk told me that snakes are very dangerous to mice."

"That's silly gossip," said Hedgehog. "You know Snake would never hurt you. Come on. We can walk together, and you will be **perfectly** safe."

Mouse hesitated.

"I insist," said Hedgehog.

So Mouse went along.

Hedgehog talked about little things, but Mouse wasn't paying attention. He was still worrying about Snake. He looked around **nervously**.

He looked everywhere but at his feet.

"Ohhhhhh... HELP!"

Hedgehog peered down.

"You should be afraid of yourself, Mouse, not of Snake."

"It's not funny," Mouse yelled. "I've hurt my foot and I can't get out."

"Are you sure?" Hedgehog shouted.

"Yes!" Mouse yelled.

"Stay calm," said Hedgehog. "I'll get help."

Just then Squirrel walked by.

"Mouse has gotten it into his head to be afraid of Snake," said Hedgehog. "He was so nervous that he didn't watch where he was going. He fell into a hole and hurt his foot, and now he can't get out. Can you help?"

But Squirrel couldn't help.

"It will be too dark," she said, "and there might be spiders."

Rabbit came along, and Hedgehog told him about Mouse and Snake.

"You know how to go down holes," said Hedgehog.

Rabbit looked into the hole. "Hello, Mouse!" he yelled.

"It's too deep," Rabbit said to Hedgehog, "and the walls are too straight. I wouldn't be able to hop out."

"Why don't *you* go, Hedgehog?" asked Squirrel.

"Because Mouse would have to get on my back, and my prickles would hurt him," Hedgehog said.

Mouse started to cry.

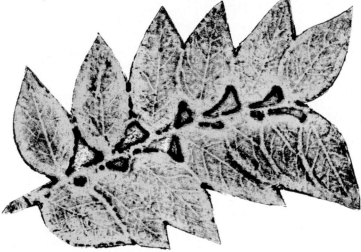

STOP AND CHECK

Visualize How might Mouse feel at the bottom of the hole? Use the Visualize strategy to help you understand where Mouse is.

Wishywishywishy...

Hedgehog heard the grass move.

It was Snake.

"What's going on?" said Snake.

"Shhhhh!" Hedgehog whispered. "Mouse fell into a deep, dark hole. He hurt his foot and he can't get out."

"Is it a **secret**?" Snake whispered back.

"Not exactly," whispered Hedgehog. "It's just that we don't know how to get him out. Squirrel is afraid to go down by herself, Rabbit wouldn't be able to hop out, and I'm too prickly."

"Then I'll go down," Snake said. "No problem."

"Oh, no," said Hedgehog. "That's not a good idea at all."

"Not at all," said Squirrel.

"Not at all," said Rabbit.

"You see, Snake," Hedgehog said, "Fox told Skunk and Skunk told Mouse that snakes are dangerous to mice. Mouse was trying to hide from *you* when he fell into the hole."

"But I have always been Mouse's friend," said Snake.

"Of course you have," said Hedgehog.

"So I am going to **rescue** Mouse anyway," said Snake.

"How will you do it without scaring Mouse?"
asked Hedgehog.

"Someone get a stick,"
said Snake.

Squirrel did it.

"Now tie my tail around it,"
said Snake.

Rabbit did it.

"Now make sure the
knot is tight."

Hedgehog did it.

"Now watch!"

When Mouse saw the stick,
he grabbed it.

Snake began to climb the tree,
and slowly Mouse came up.

Mouse saw Snake and gasped.

Then he saw the stick still tied to Snake's tail.

"Snake saved you," said Hedgehog.

"He did," said Squirrel.

"He rescued you," said Rabbit.

"Because I would never hurt you," Snake said.

Mouse turned a deep shade of pink.

"I am very sorry," he said.

Snake, Squirrel, Hedgehog, and Rabbit helped Mouse
hobble home.

They bandaged Mouse's foot, and he lay down to rest.

STOP AND CHECK

Visualize What happens after Mouse gets out of the hole? What does that tell you about the animals? Use the Visualize strategy to help you.

Several mornings later, Hedgehog was
taking his walk, and along came Mouse.
He was holding a bouquet of flowers.

"Where are you going?"
asked Hedgehog.

"I'm going to say thank you to Snake,"
said Mouse, "and to give him some
flowers that I picked."

And Snake was very pleased to have them.

About the Author and Illustrator

HOLLY KELLER loved to read and draw when she was little. Now she writes and illustrates her own books.

Holly tried something new to make the pictures for *Help! A Story of Friendship*. Holly made a collage, a picture made from different materials. She used cardboard, paper, and other things to create the animals. For Snake, she used an onion bag. Holly even used cupcake liners to make Squirrel!

Author's Purpose

On page 14, the drawing makes you look down into the hole. On page 17, you look up from the bottom of the hole. Why do you think Holly changed how the reader looks at the drawing on the page?

Corey Keller

Respond to the Text

Summarize

Use important details to summarize the story. Information from your Key Details chart may help you.

Details	Details	Details

Write

How does the author use illustrations to show how talking about others can affect a friendship? Use these sentence starters:

Mouse believed...
Snake felt...

Make Connections

How do the animal friends depend on each other?
ESSENTIAL QUESTION

How can friends help you solve a problem or do something you can't do by yourself?
TEXT TO WORLD

Compare Texts
Read about two friends
who know how to share.

32

Crayons

By Helen H. Moore

I had a box of crayons,
All shiny, straight and new.

I lent a friend the red one,
And — oops — it broke in two!

My friend said she was sorry,
But I said, "I don't care,

'Cause now we both can color
With one crayon — we can share!"

Make Connections

How do these friends **depend** on each other? ESSENTIAL QUESTION

Think about the **actions** of all the friends you read about this week. How do friends treat each other? TEXT TO TEXT

Helen H. Moore

Genre • Realistic Fiction

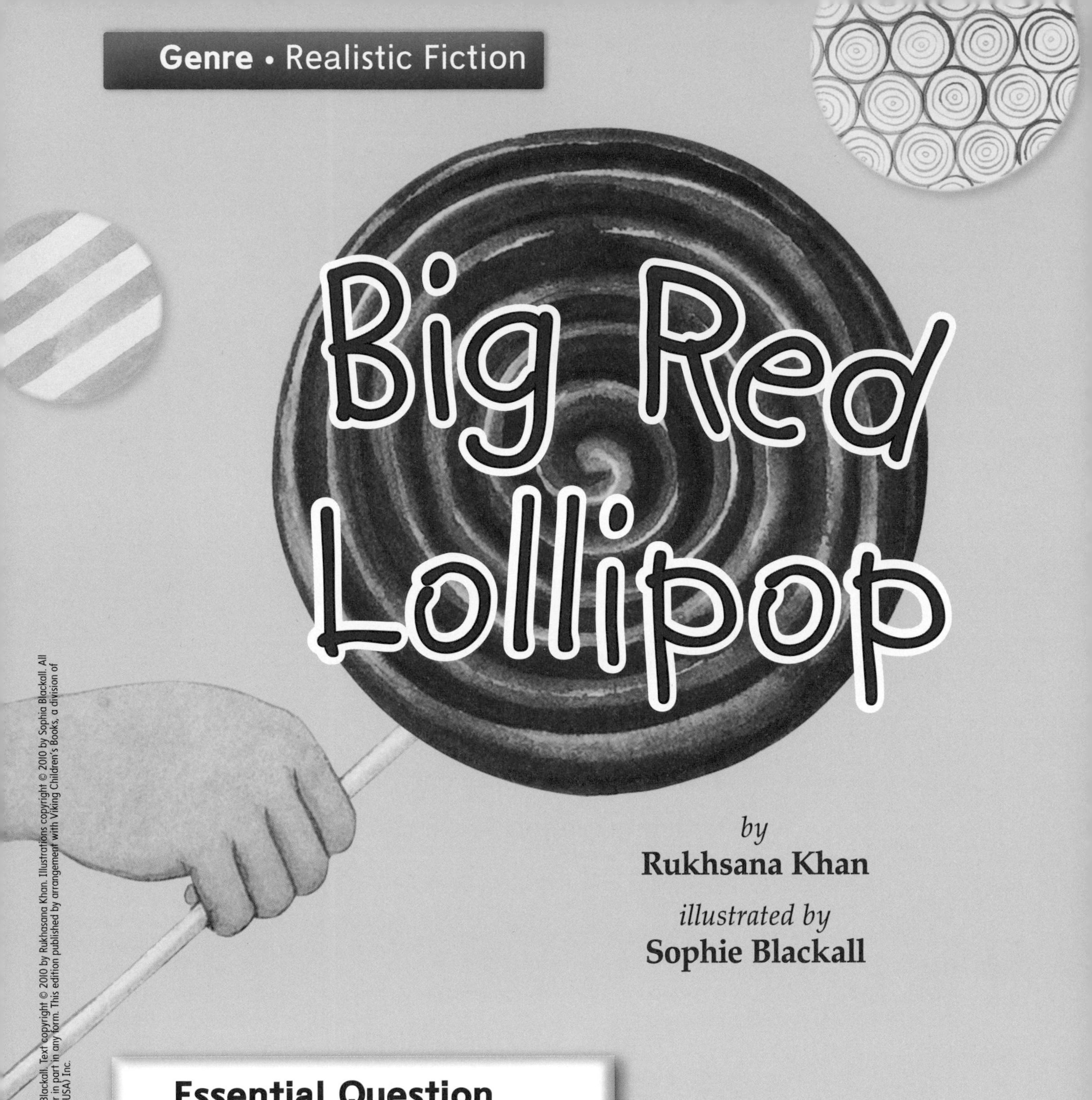

Big Red Lollipop

by
Rukhsana Khan

illustrated by
Sophie Blackall

Essential Question

How are families around the world the same and different?

Read about how a girl and her sisters get along.

Go Digital!

I'm so excited I run all the way home from school.

"Ami! I've been **invited** to a birthday party!
There's going to be games and toys, cake and ice cream!
Can I go?"

Sana screams, "I wanna go too!"

Ami says, "What's a birthday party?"

"It's when they celebrate the day they were born."

"Why do they do *that*?"

"They just do! Can I go?"

Sana screams, "I wanna go too!"

"I can't take *her*! She's not invited."

"Why not?" says Ami.

"They don't do that here!"

Ami says, "Well that's not **fair**. You call up your friend and ask if you can bring Sana, or else you can't go."

"But Ami! They'll laugh at me! They'll never invite me to another party again!"

Sana screams, "I wanna go too!"

I say, "Look, Sana, one day you'll get invited to your own friends' parties. Wouldn't you like that better?"

"No! I wanna go now!"

I beg and **plead**, but Ami won't listen. I have no choice. I have to call. Sally says, "All right." But it doesn't sound all right. I know she thinks I'm weird.

At the party, I'm the only one who brought her little sister. Sana has to win all the games, and when she falls down during musical chairs, she cries like a baby.

Before we leave the party, Sally's mom gives us little bags.

Inside there are chocolates and candies, a whistle, a ruby ring, and a big red lollipop! Sana eats her big red lollipop on the way home in the car. I save mine for later.

Sana doesn't know how to make things last. By bedtime, her candies are all gone, her whistle is broken, and the ruby in her ring is missing. I put my big red lollipop on the top shelf of the fridge to have in the morning.

All night I dream about how good it will taste.

In the morning, I get up early to have it. Sana's already up. When she sees me, she runs away.

I open the fridge door. All that's left of my lollipop is a triangle stuck to a stick.

"SANA!"

STOP AND CHECK

Visualize What happened to the lollipop? What does that tell you about Sana? Use the Visualize strategy to help you.

I hear a sound in the front hall closet. I should have known. That's where she always hides.

I shove **aside** the coats and boots. "I'm going to *get* you!"

Quick as a rat, she scoots through my legs and runs around and around the living room, the dining room, the kitchen, yelling, "Ami! Ami! Help! Help!"

Ami comes out, rubbing her eyes. Sana runs behind Ami, where I can't get her.

"What's going on out here?" says Ami.

Sana says, "Rubina's trying to get me!"

Ami puts her hands on her hips. "Are you trying to get your little sister again?"

"She ate my *lollipop*! The greedy thing! She ate it!"

Ami says, "For shame! It's just a lollipop! Can't you **share** with your little sister?"

I want to cry, but I don't.

Sana runs to the fridge and brings back the triangle stuck to the stick. "Look! I didn't eat *all* of your lollipop! I left the triangle for you!"

"See?" says Ami. "She didn't eat *all* of it. She's sharing with you! Go ahead. Take the triangle."

So I have to take it.

"Go ahead. *Eat* the triangle."

But I don't. With all my might, I throw it across the room. It skitters under the sofa.

Sana **scurries** after it and eats that too.

The worst thing is that all the girls at school know if they invite me to their birthday parties, I have to bring Sana.

I don't get any invitations for a really long time.

Then one day Sana comes home waving an invitation. "Ami! I've been invited to a birthday party! There's going to be games and toys and cake and ice cream! Can I go?"

Our little sister Maryam screams, "I wanna go too!"

Sana says, "No! I can't take *her!* She's not invited!"

STOP AND CHECK

Visualize What do you think will happen if Sana takes Maryam to the party? Use the Visualize strategy to help you.

49

Ami says, "Well . . . it's only fair. You went to Rubina's friend's party, now Rubina and Maryam can go to your friend's party."

I say, "Leave me out of it."

Ami says, "Fine then, you have to take Maryam."

Now it's Sana's turn to beg and plead. Ami won't listen. Sana's begging so hard she's crying, but still Ami won't listen.

I *could* just watch her have to take Maryam.
I *could* just let her make a fool of herself at that
party. I *could* just let her not be invited to any
more parties, but something makes me tap Ami
on the shoulder.

"What?"

"Don't make Sana take Maryam to the party."

"No?" says Ami.

"No," I say.

Ami thinks for a moment, then says, "Okay."

So Sana gets to go by herself.

After the party, I hear a knock on my door.

"What do *you* want?" I ask Sana.

"Here." She hands me a big green lollipop.

"This is for you."

"Thanks," I say.

After that we're friends.

About the Author and Illustrator

Rukhsana Khan was born in Pakistan. Her family moved to Canada when she was three years old. Rukhsana tells stories about other cultures as well as her own.

Sophie Blackall grew up in Australia where she learned to draw on the beach with sticks. She kept drawing because it was fun. Now she illustrates many books.

Author's Purpose

Authors write stories for different reasons. Sometimes they want to tell a funny story. Sometimes they want readers to learn a lesson. Why do you think Rukhsana wrote this story?

Respond to the Text

Summarize

Use important details about the characters, setting, and events to summarize the story. Information from your Character, Setting, and Events chart may help you.

Character	Setting	Events

Write

How does Rubina's relationship with her sister, Sana, change from the beginning of the story to the end? Use these sentence frames:

> At the beginning of the story, Rubina feels.....
> At the end, Rubina feels......

Make Connections

How are families around the world the same and different? **ESSENTIAL QUESTION**

How can brothers and sisters work to get along? **TEXT TO WORLD**

Compare Texts
Read about how families are
alike and different.

A Look at Families

Families around the world do some things the same. They have differences, too. Let's take a look at how families in different **cultures** live.

All families need homes. Some families live in large cities. They might live in tall apartment buildings. Many families live in the same building.

Some families live near water. Some families live in houses on stilts. Stilts are tall poles. They keep the homes safe from water.

**Apartment homes in the
United States and Denmark**

Family homes in Chile

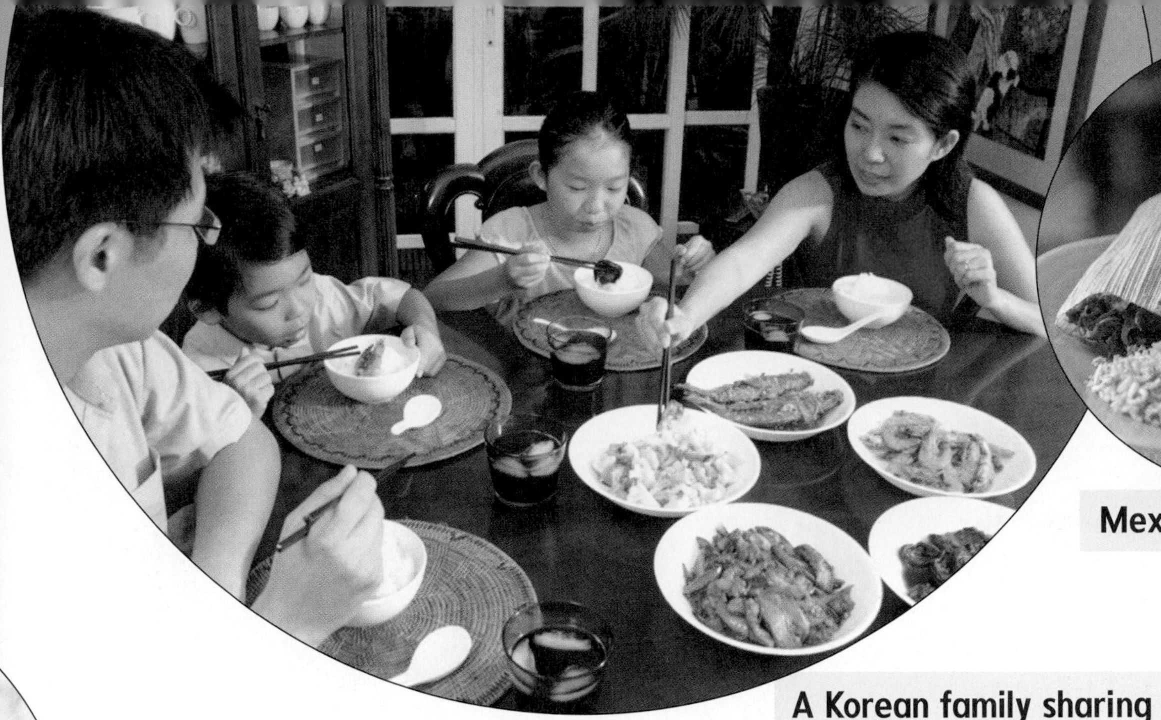

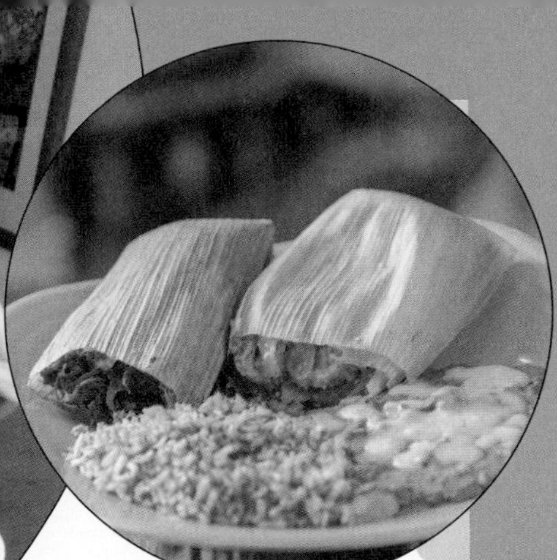

Mexican meal

A Korean family sharing a meal

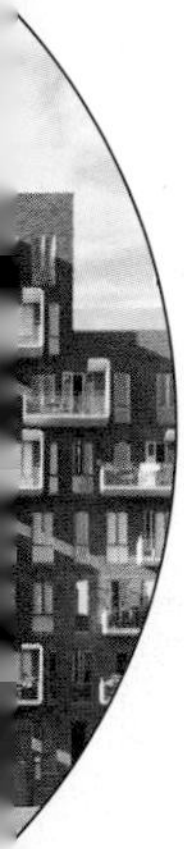

All families share food. Culture has a lot to do with what a family eats. Families may also eat foods from other cultures.

Some families in Korea eat rice and fish. Meals in Mexico often include rice and beans. Pasta is a common Italian meal.

Pasta meal

(tl) Asia Images Group/Getty Images (tr) BestStockFoto/Shutterstock.com (b) BananaStock/PunchStock

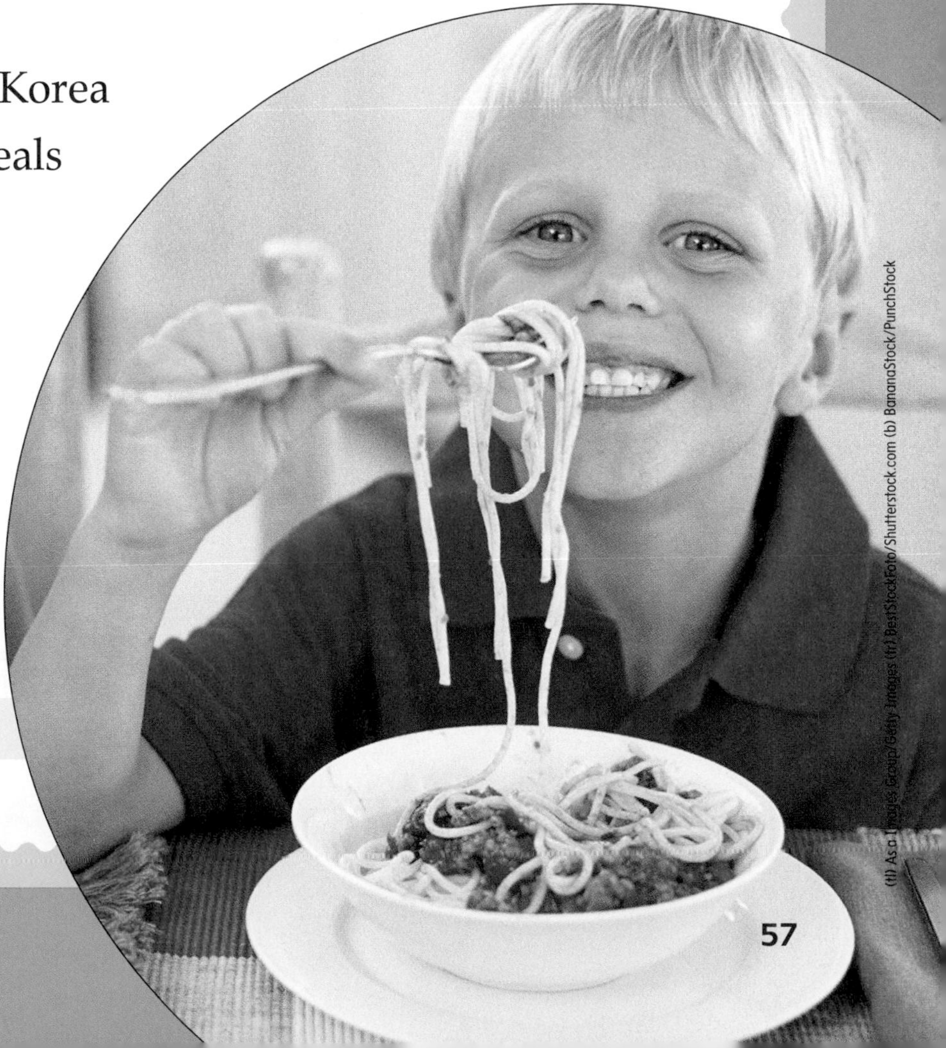

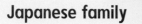

Japanese family

All families talk to each other. Different families speak different **languages.** Culture has a lot to do with how families talk to each other.

In Japanese, a grandfather may be called *ojiisan* (oh-jee-sahn). A grandmother may be *obaasan* (oh-baah-sahn).

In South Africa when families visit each other, they say, "Sawubona!" (sah-woo-boh-na). This means hello!

South African family

Indian family

American family

All families celebrate together. In India, families celebrate the holiday *Diwali*. They light a row of lamps called *deepa* (dee-pah) outside their homes. In the United States, families celebrate Independence Day. They might watch fireworks or go to a parade.

What are some things you celebrate with your family?

Make Connections

How are families around the world the same and different? ESSENTIAL QUESTION

How do all the families you have read about this week celebrate together? TEXT TO TEXT

Essential Question

How can a pet be an important friend?

Read about a boy who has a special pet fish.

Go Digital!

Your Fish and You

60

NOT NORMAN
A Goldfish Story

By Kelly Bennett

Illustrated by Noah Z. Jones

When I got Norman, I didn't want to keep him. I wanted a **different** kind of pet.

Not Norman.

I wanted a pet who could run and catch.
Or one who could climb trees and chase strings.
A soft, furry pet to sleep on my bed at night.

Not Norman.

All Norman does is swim around and around
and around and around and around and
around and around and around. . . .

"This is it, Norman," I **decide**. "I'm trading you for a good pet." Norman doesn't move. Not even a fin twitches.

How can I **trade** him like this? No one will want a sorry-looking fish in a gunky bowl.

When I drop Norman into his nice, clean bowl, he starts dipping and flipping, flapping his fins around. He looks so goofy I have to laugh.

"Don't think that just because you made me laugh, I'm going to keep you," I tell him. "Tomorrow, you're outta here."

Norman blows a stream of bubbles.

The next day, I take Norman to school with me. If I talk him up real good during Show-and-Tell, maybe someone will want him.

On the way there, we see my friend Austin. Austin has a real cool dog—and seven puppies. "Wanna swap one of your pups for Norman?" I ask. "Who's Norman?" asks Austin. "My goldfish," I say.

By the time I rescue Norman, half his water is gone!

"I'm sorry," I tell Norman when we get to school. "I'm really sorry." He just **stares** at me all googly-eyed.

Finally it's my turn to Show-and-Tell. Just as I start to talk about goldfish, Emily shouts, "Jenny's gone! Who let my snake loose?"

69

Does anyone hear the story of how I got Norman?
Does anyone even ask to hold his bowl? No. They're
all jumping and screaming and chasing the snake.
Not Norman. He's looking right at me.

"Thanks for listening," I tell him.

STOP AND CHECK

Ask and Answer Questions Why doesn't anyone
listen to the boy telling his stories about Norman?
Go back to the text to find the answer.

71

That afternoon, we go to my music lesson. As soon as it's over, I'm taking Norman back to the pet store.

I take out my tuba and begin to play.

Bom bom bom baaaa Ba ba ba boooo Bo bo bo beeee.

I **glance** over at Norman. He's swaying back and forth. *Glu glu glu glug,* he mouths.

"Look! Norman's singing," I say. "Pay attention!" snaps Maestro. "And *try* to play the **proper** notes."

Maestro makes me stay for extra practice. By the time my lesson is over, it's too late to go to the pet store. "Don't think that just because you like my music, I'm going to keep you," I tell Norman.

He glugs.

That night I'm sound asleep when . . . SCREECH, SCRITCH! What's that noise?

SCRATCH SCRITCH SCREEEECH! Yikes, there's something at the window!

Then, out of the corner of my eye, I spot . . .

Norman!

He isn't scared. He isn't swimming around in circles either. He glugs and gives me a little wave.

I'm not alone.

Together, Norman and I slide open the curtains. It was just a broken tree branch.

"Thanks for watching out for me, Norman."

STOP AND CHECK

Visualize How does Norman help the boy not feel alone? Use the Visualize strategy to help you.

On Saturday, I take Norman to the pet store, just like I said I would. I look at the cats and dogs and snakes and birds. I look at the hamsters and mice and lizards, too.

They all look like good pets, but they are . . .

Not Norman.

When I got Norman, I wasn't sure I wanted to keep him. But now, even if I could pick any pet in the whole world, I wouldn't trade him.

Not Norman.

About the Author and Illustrator

KELLY BENNETT wrote *Not Norman* because of her own pet goldfish. "I write what I know about—friendship, pets, family life," says Kelly, "but I also write about things I want to know about." She gets ideas from adventures with her family.

NOAH Z. JONES currently lives in sunny Los Angeles, California, with his family. He has illustrated many books. Now he is working on a cartoon series.

Author's Purpose

Kelly uses words such as *bom bom bom baaaa*. These words sound like a tuba. Using words that sound like the object or action they refer to is called *onomatopoeia*. What other sound words does Kelly use to tell the story?

Respond to the Text

Summarize

Use important details to summarize how a goldfish becomes the best pet in the world. Information from your chart may help you.

Character	Setting	Events

Write

How does the author show how the boy's relationship with Norman changes from the beginning of the story to the end? Use these sentence starters:

The boy really wants a...
In school, the boy...

Make Connections

How can a pet fish be an important friend?
ESSENTIAL QUESTION

Think about what you learned in this story. How can a pet be a good friend? TEXT TO WORLD

Genre · Poetry

Compare Texts
Read about a special **friendship** between a girl and her pet puppy.

My Puppy

By Aileen Fisher

It's funny
My puppy
Knows just how I feel.

When I'm happy,
He's yappy
And squirms like an eel!

When I'm grumpy,
He's slumpy
And stays at my heel.

It's funny my puppy
Knows such a great deal.

Make Connections

How is this puppy an important friend?
ESSENTIAL QUESTION

Tell about the other **relationships** between pets and their owners you read about this week. **TEXT TO TEXT**

Lola and Tiva:
An Unlikely Friendship

Told by **JULIANA, ISABELLA,** *and* **CRAIG HATKOFF**

Photos by **Peter Greste**

Essential Question
How do we care for animals?

Read about a girl who cares for her pet rhino.

Go Digital!

There is a very special place in Kenya, Africa, called the Lewa Wildlife Conservancy. Lewa is a large place where animals **roam** free, and people – called rangers – watch over them. A young girl named Tiva lived there with her family. Her father worked for Lewa.

Everyone at Lewa knew that Tiva had always wanted a puppy. But puppies were not **allowed**. Instead the people at Lewa found Tiva a different kind of friend—a young black rhino named Lola. Lola seemed to work just as well as a puppy for Tiva. Lola and Tiva became the best of friends. This is their true story.

Lola was born at Lewa to a mother that was blind. For a couple of days Lola drank her mother's milk for food and stayed close by. But when she was strong enough to walk, Lola **wandered** off to another area of Lewa. Her mother could not see Lola walking away. Without her mother to feed and protect her, Lola was in danger.

Animals roam free at Lewa.

Lola needed food and could become a meal for a lion or
another hungry animal. She could not find her mother
and her blind mother could not find her. The rangers who
worked at Lewa searched for Lola. When they found her,
they brought her to a **safe** place in Lewa that was near
Tiva's house. There, Lola would be out of danger.

Tiva was **excited** when Lola arrived. She wanted to take **care** of Lola. Like any baby, Lola needed many things. Most of all, Lola was hungry and needed milk. Tiva learned to feed Lola. Lola drank a bottle five times a day. Each time, she drank over a gallon!

Tiva loved Lola. Lola was a lot like a big puppy.

She tried to climb things. She licked things.
She smelled things.

Lola begged at the dinner table.

STOP AND CHECK

Ask and Answer Questions How was Lola like a big puppy? Go back to the text to find the answer.

Like most pets, Lola never posed when Tiva tried to take pictures. She wanted to nap.

But Lola did like for Tiva to pet her between the ears.

Of course, rhinos are not really like dogs. They don't eat dog food. When Lola was about five months old, she started to eat like a real rhino. She ate shrubs, twigs, and leaves. Her upper lip is shaped like a hook and can grab onto food. Lola could wrap her hook around sticks and leaves. But she still loved to drink her milk, too.

Rhinos in the **wild** are usually shy. They often run away if they see or smell people. Lola was too young to be afraid of people. Tiva and the rangers became her family.

A baby rhino is called a calf. A calf usually stays with its mother for two years. The mother watches over her calf. Lola needed someone to look after her. Tiva became Lola's special friend.

Like a pet, Lola needed special care. Tiva helped pick bugs off Lola's body. The bugs could make Lola sick. In the wild, birds eat the bugs off a rhino's skin. But birds would not do that for Lola. There were too many people around.

Lola also needed to take baths. Mud baths! When a rhino rolls in the mud, it is called wallowing. It is an important part of being a rhino.

The mud protects the rhino's skin from the sun – like sunscreen. Once the mud dries, it also keeps bugs from biting.

Tiva made sure Lola knew how to wallow. It isn't as easy as it looks. It takes a lot of practice.

A rhino does not have to wash the mud off. A little girl does.

Lola and Tiva shared their days together.

Lola learned about being a rhinoceros. Tiva learned about being a friend.

It was a lot of fun, and it wore them out.

Now Lola is almost full-grown. She is too big to play with Tiva like she used to.

But the time they spent together will always be special. After all, a little girl never forgets her first best friend.

STOP AND CHECK

Ask and Answer Questions How have Lola and Tiva changed? Go back to the text to find the answer.

A Letter from Juliana, Isabella, and Craig Hatkoff

To Our Readers:

What does a little girl who lives in Africa do if she can't have a pet dog? She takes in a pet rhino! That is if she lives on a nature conservancy like Tiva did. When we first saw the photographs of Lola and Tiva playing together, we fell in love with their story. We think it is every young animal lover's dream: to feed, take care of, and be friends with a wild animal. We hope you enjoy the true story of Lola and Tiva as much as we do.

With hope and peace,

Craig, Juliana, and Isabella Hatkoff

Peter Greste

Peter likes to take photos for news stories. One story he photographed told of the friendship between a baby hippo and a giant tortoise.

Author's Purpose

Authors write for a reason, or purpose. Why do you think the authors wrote this book? Support your answer with examples from the text.

Respond to the Text

Summarize

Use details to summarize the needs of a young black rhino. Tell how Tiva helped to meet those needs. Information from your Key Details chart may help you.

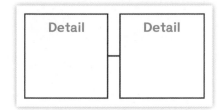

Write

How does the author use details in the text and pictures to show that Tiva was a good friend to Lola? Use these sentence frames:

In the photos I see...

The text shows...

Make Connections

How did Tiva and her family care for Lola?
ESSENTIAL QUESTION

What other friendships between animals and people do you know about? Tell a partner about how the friends cared for each other.
TEXT TO WORLD

Compare Texts
Read about how people at animal shelters care for animals.

Animal Needs

Anne is in charge of an animal shelter. We asked her questions about how people **care** for animals there. In this interview the words after **Q:** are the questions we asked. The words after **A:** are Anne's answers.

Anne is the owner of Our Animal Friends.

Q: What is an animal shelter?

A: An animal shelter is a place for animals that need an owner to take care of them.

Q: What kinds of animals live at the shelter?

A: We have dogs, cats, and rabbits.

Q: How do you make sure all the animals have their **needs** met?

A: It isn't easy! All animals need food, water, air, and shelter. Each animal has different needs. Some animals, such as dogs, like to eat meat. Other animals, such

A puppy's needs are different from a dog's needs. To grow, the puppy needs to eat more times during the day.

as rabbits, eat plants. Dogs need exercise. I take them for walks on a leash. If I did that with one of our cats, the cat would not be happy! I would not be giving it the care it needs.

Q: Who else works at the shelter?

A: We have an animal doctor, a veterinarian. He makes sure the animals are healthy.

Make Connections

How do we care for animals?
ESSENTIAL QUESTION

Think about the animals you have read about this week. How are their needs the same? **TEXT TO TEXT**

Families Working Together

? Essential Question

What happens when families work together?

Read about a family that works together on a farm.

Go Digital!

How does a family farm work?

It's 3:45 a.m. on Tuesday. Mary Gelder is ready for work. She and her mom drive many miles from their farm in Michigan to Chicago. They sell fruits and vegetables at a farmer's market. **Customers** visit their farm stand to buy fresh food. "I love seeing who will eat the food my family works hard to grow," Mary says. After a long day, the Gelders return home. They do it all again on Saturday.

But their work does not stop there. Each day, they do many **chores**. The family plants, waters, and picks fruits and vegetables.

STOP AND CHECK

Ask and Answer Questions What work does the Gelder family do each Tuesday? Go back to the text to find the answer.

One of Mary's **jobs** is to care for the chickens. Her brothers repair trucks and tractors. They **check** farm **tools**, such as shovels and drills. Mary's mom, René, takes care of money and workers.

When the Gelders **choose** what to plant, they look at demand. In the summer, people want strawberries. So the family plants a lot of them. Sometimes, they sell less than they have.

The Gelders turn the extra fruit into jam. "I love strawberries!" Mary says. "It's great to have jam in the winter, when there is no supply of fresh strawberries."

Producing and Consuming

Some people produce items that people buy. People who buy items are called consumers. Here's a look at some items that are produced and who consumes them.

What's Produced	Who Consumes It?
Bicycles	Kids and Athletes
Books	Teachers, Students, Readers
Food	People and Animals
Cars	Drivers

The Gelder family farm produces apples and other fruits.

People buy jam and fresh food from the Gelder family's farm stand.

Running a farm **costs** money, so the Gelders try to save. Some time ago, they bought an outdoor wood stove. They burn the farm's old trees for heat. The heat warms their home and barn. It helped the family **spend** less during the cold months. "We help each other and we help the environment," René says. "I'm really proud of my family and our farm!"

Respond to the Text

1. Use details from the selection to summarize. SUMMARIZE

2. How does the family farm help provide other people with food? WRITE

3. How does the Gelder family's work on their farm help others? TEXT TO WORLD

Compare Texts

Read about why people make goods and provide services.

Why We Work

Look around you. The things you see have been produced, or made by a person at work. These things are called goods.

Some people have jobs that provide or offer services. Services are actions that people do.

Police officers and firefighters provide the service of helping others.

Workers in factories produce goods like cars that people buy.

Some service jobs include a teacher or a food server. A teacher provides the service of helping students learn. A food server brings food to your table at a restaurant.

When people make goods or provide services, they earn money. They can use the money to buy more goods and services that **cost** money. People who buy things are consumers.

Items you must have to live are needs, like food or clothing. Sometimes, you wish for other things. These are wants, such as games or books.

Will you create goods? Or will you provide services? The choice is yours!

Make Connections

What happens when people work together? ESSENTIAL QUESTION

How do people work together so you can buy things? TEXT TO TEXT

Sled Dogs Run

By JONATHAN LONDON

Illustrated by JON VAN ZYLE

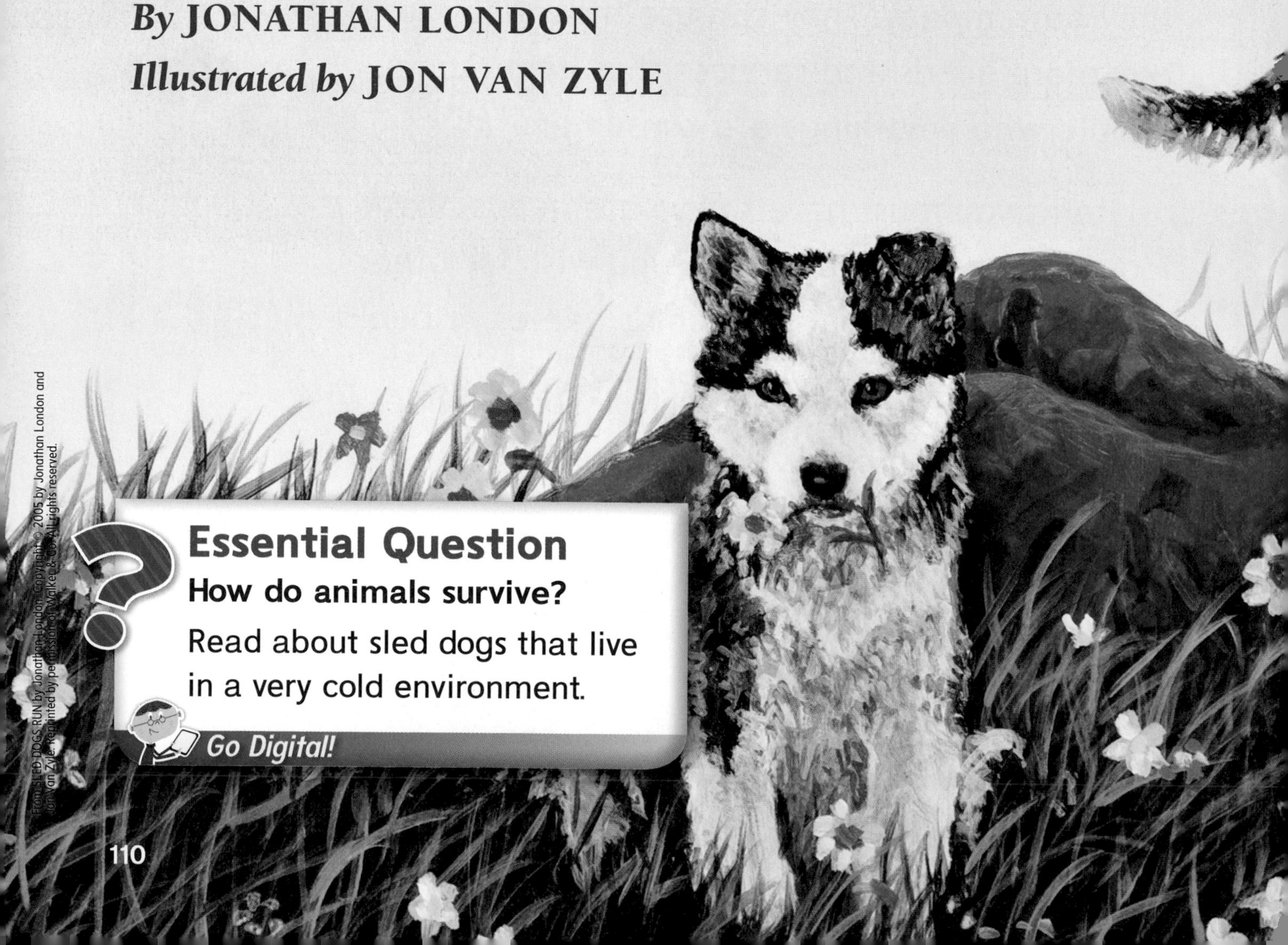

Essential Question
How do animals survive?
Read about sled dogs that live in a very cold environment.

Go Digital!

They were born in the spring:
fat, tumbling puppy balls
full of **fresh** puppy smell
and puppy life.

There was Skookum and Hawk and Bamboo.
Here in Alaska, in the Far North, *Skookum* means "smart."
"See how Hawk and Bamboo chase him but can't
catch him," says Papa. "He will be the leader."

Now, in summer, the training begins.
Sled dogs run. That's what they live for.
To run. To run and pull.

First, they wear a harness, to get used to it.
Then they pull a small log, bouncing and skidding
behind them.

In the fall, they pull a cart for the first time.

Papa runs behind me. I call out: "Skookum! Hawk! Bamboo! Good dogs!" For now, they run with older dogs. I can't wait till the first snow.

STOP AND CHECK

Make Predictions What do you think will happen at the first snow? Use the Make Predictions strategy to help you.

115

In the winter, the snow comes.
White on white, as soft as owl's feathers.
I lie down in the softness and make a snow angel,
but my dogs are **eager** to run.

And by February, they are ready to pull as a team—
with me as musher. My first solo run! Mama heats
up a sloppy stew. The dogs must eat fast before it freezes.

Mama gives me a hug. "You will love the
quiet," she says, "and the oneness with nature."
"You will love the speed," Papa says, "and the
sense of **freedom**."

When I come with the harnesses,
the dogs go crazy.
They run in circles,
howling and crying and yipping with joy.

Hitched to the gang line,
they are raring to go.
Mama says, "Be back by dark!"
In the North, in the winter, dark comes early.
Papa says, "Trust the dogs.
They will know the way!"

I pull the snow hook and shout, "Hike!"
The sled feels like it's leaving the ground.
Whoosh! We're off—the dogs straining,
tugging, running out before me, huffing puffs
of breath.

We are racing cloud shadows.
We are racing a snowy owl.
We are racing the wind.

We spook a snowshoe hare
and fly after it.
The sled whips.
The runners *shusshh*.
The collars and snaps jingle.
Hare disappears into white.

The dogs smell moose
and go after it.
Moose stops and turns around—
fire in her eyes.
With one kick, a moose can cave in a rib
cage. That's what Papa says.

I yell "Haw!" and my dogs swerve left,
away from the moose.
I yell "Gee!" and my dogs swerve right,
their keen noses scenting the trail.

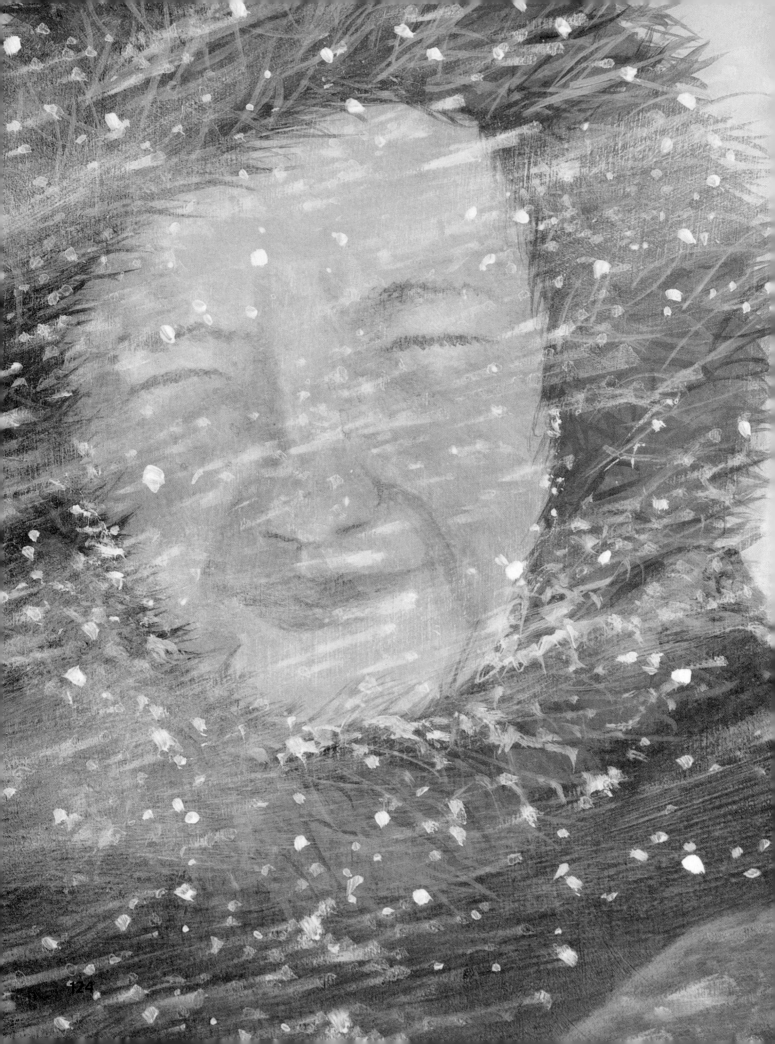

I hear a howl.
Is it the howl of wolves?
The hair stands up on my dogs' necks.

No, it is the howling wind blowing the snow sideways.
I hang on to the sled handle for dear life.
The storm is a hungry wolf, eating up the light.
Just as we hit a frozen lake we are blinded.
We are lost.

STOP AND CHECK

Ask and Answer Questions What does the girl mean when she says that they are "blinded"? Go back to the text to find the answer.

But I remember what Papa says:
"Trust the dogs.
They will know the way!"
The dogs are my eyes.

Through the snow-blind world we drive.
All I hear is the howl of the wind—
and the boom of the lake ice shifting.
"Skookum! Hawk! Bamboo! Take me home!"

Suddenly the wind dies to a whisper,
and the air clears, like a clean window.
"Whoa!" I call. We come to a stop.
"Good dogs! Good team!"
The sun is down and the full moon is rising,
tipping its golden light.

When my dogs stop panting,
there's a **silence**
as quiet as owl's breath.

Then I see, beyond the long blue
shadows of the spruce: lights.
Our cabin in the woods!
Home.
And we become a part of the
night and the moon and the snow
and the trees and we run.

"Skookum! Hawk! Bamboo! Hike!"

We run to keep up with our hearts.

About the Author and Illustrator

Jonathan London and his sons love to go to "wild, snowy places." Jonathan started writing by making up stories for his children. Many of his stories are about nature and wild animals.

Jon van Zyle is the official artist of the Iditarod Sled Dog Race. This famous race goes 1,049 miles through the Alaskan wilderness each winter. Jon owns twenty Siberian huskies!

Author's Purpose

Jonathan uses words like *softness* and *yipping with joy* in the story. These words describe things. How do they help you visualize what you are reading?

Respond to the Text

Summarize

Use important details about the characters, setting, and plot to summarize the story. Information from your Plot chart may help you.

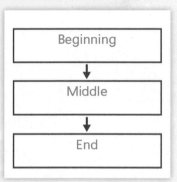

Write

How does the girl learn to trust her dogs on the first run? Use these sentence starters:

When she is in the storm, the girl feels...
Then she remembers...

Make Connections

How do animals survive in extreme environments?
ESSENTIAL QUESTION

What can you learn from *Sled Dogs Run* about trust?
TEXT TO WORLD

Compare Texts
Read about one animal that lives in extreme cold and one that lives in extreme heat.

Cold Dog, Hot Fox

There is a very cold place in Asia. It is called Siberia. The **climate** there is harsh. In winter, the temperature is far below freezing. The wind is strong. Few animals can live there because of the weather conditions.

Siberian Husky

The Siberian husky is a kind of dog. It has body parts that help it **adapt** to very cold places. When the wind and snow blow, the dog squints its eyes. Even with its eyes almost closed it can still see.

A husky's fur has two parts. The bottom part is very short hair. The top part is long hair. The longer hair keeps water off the dog's body. It works like a warm raincoat.

The dog's tail is bushy. A husky can wrap its tail around its face when it goes to sleep. Its tail keeps its face warm.

If you look at the bottom of a husky's paw, you see thick black pads and fur. The paws help the dog stay warm.

The Siberian husky looks like other dogs. But it has special features that help it live in cold places.

Parts of a Husky

Tail is furry.

Eyes have a special shape.

Ears have fur.

Fur is thick.

Paws have fur.

(t) Jason Edwards/National Geographic/Getty Images (b) Per Breiehagen/The Image Bank/Getty Images

Life in the Heat

The Sahara desert is in Africa. Summers there are very hot and dry. Few animals can live there.

Fennec Fox

A fennec fox has body parts that help it live in the hot, dry desert.

The fox has big ears. They help extra heat leave the fox's body. The fox's ears also have hairs that trap sand. The sand does not blow in the fox's ears.

The fox has thick fur. The fur is the color of sand. The fox also has a furry tail. It wraps its tail around its body to protect itself from the heat.

A fennec fox is nocturnal. It sleeps during the day. It eats at night.

The fox's feet have hair on the bottom. The hair protects the fox's feet from the hot sand. The fox also uses its feet as a tool. It digs holes in the ground and stays in the hole during the day. The fox comes out at night when it is cooler.

All of these features help the fennec fox live in the desert.

Parts of a Fox

Ears help the fox lose body heat.

Fur is thick.

Paws have fur. Their shape helps the fox dig.

Tail is furry.

Make Connections

How do these animals survive in very cold and hot places? **ESSENTIAL QUESTION**

Think about the animals you have read about this week. How do their bodies help them survive? **TEXT TO TEXT**

WOLF! WOLF!

JOHN ROCCO

WOLF'S PEAS

? Essential Question

What can animals in stories teach us?

Read a different version of the story of the boy who cried wolf.

Go Digital!

The hungry old wolf was too slow to **snatch** birds and too stiff to chase rabbits, so he tried growing food in a small garden.

"Bah, weeds everywhere! There are so many I can't even find the vegetables." The old wolf growled, rubbing his empty stomach.

As he yanked dandelions from where his carrots should have been, his ears began to twitch.

"WOLF! WOLF!"

The old wolf fumbled with his hearing aid.

Who's calling me? I don't remember having any friends on this mountain.

In fact, the old wolf didn't have any friends on any mountain.

"Maybe they have some food to share? A mere morsel would do," he said.

His bones creaked and his joints cracked as he slowly made his way toward the voice.

After a tiring climb and two stubbed toes, the old wolf came to a clearing.

"What's this? A boy? With goats!" The old wolf drooled with excitement. "Surely he can spare *one* for a hungry wolf."

Before he could step into the meadow, a group of villagers came clambering up the hillside.

The old wolf stayed hidden behind the bamboo as the villagers surrounded the boy.

"Where's the wolf?" a villager cried out, waving a stick.

"Did he take any goats?" another gasped.

"What wolf?" the boy giggled. "There is no wolf."

"We ran up this hill for *nothing*?" the eldest wheezed.

"Call us *only* if you see a wolf," scolded another.

The old wolf wasn't **fond** of angry villagers, especially ones with sticks, so he limped down to a nearby stream.

"Kids. Humph! Always playing tricks on old folks and old wolves." He groaned as he soaked his tired feet.

Before long the boy's cry came again.

"WOLF! WOLF! The wolf is taking the goats!"

Another wolf is taking those tasty goats?

The old wolf couldn't stand the thought and quickly hobbled back to the meadow.

The villagers were already there, huffing and puffing from running up the hill.

"Where is the wolf? Are the goats okay?" the villagers gasped.

"What wolf?" The boy laughed.

From behind a tree, the old wolf watched the villagers stagger back down the hill.

There's got to be a way to get one of those scrumptious goats from that trickster, he thought. Perhaps through a trick of my own.

STOP AND CHECK

Make Predictions
What do you think the Wolf's trick will be? Use the Make Predictions strategy to predict what will happen.

The old wolf sat down to work out a plan and was soon snoring away and dreaming of mu shu goat and double-goat dumplings.

"WOLF! WOLF!" the boy yelled out again.

"Aaargh! I can't even enjoy the goats in my dreams! That boy is worse than weeds," the old wolf growled. He stretched his aching legs, and went to the meadow once more.

Perfect. Not a villager in sight.

The old wolf slowly crept out toward the boy. The goats swiftly scattered to the far edge of the meadow.

"Were you calling me over for lunch?" The old wolf grinned.

"WOLF! WOLF! There *is* a wolf!" the boy cried as he scrambled up a tree.

"Quit your yelling," said the wolf. Those villagers won't **believe** you, anyway."

"But this time it's true, they have to believe me. You're a *real* wolf, and you're going to take the goats."

The old wolf knew his legs were too tired to chase down goats. He carefully lowered himself onto a nearby rock and gazed up at the boy. His lips curled in a smile.

"The villagers are only going to believe you if you really are missing a goat. I can help you with that." He grinned.

"Just one goat?" The boy leaned forward on the branch.

"I'm a picky eater. That plump one looks about right. But you have to bring it to me, because if I go over there, I might change my mind and grab them all."

"Bring it to you?" the boy asked.

"On the other side of the mountain," the old wolf said, "you'll find a small garden. Just tie it to the fence post there." And he started home.

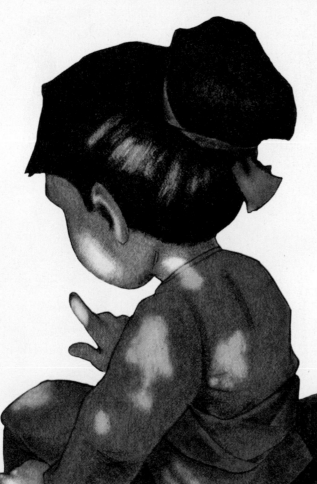

STOP AND CHECK

Confirm Predictions
Think about the prediction you made about Wolf's trick. Was it correct? How would you revise it?

151

The next morning the old wolf was overjoyed to see the plump goat nibbling away in his garden.

"Good fortune at last!" he said. "Today I'll **feast** like an old wolf should." He rubbed his paws together.

The wolf's mouth watered and his stomach grumbled as he crept up behind the goat. Suddenly he noticed something **remarkable**.

Everywhere he looked, there were ripe and juicy vegetables: baby bok choy, beautiful eggplant, ready-to-pick carrots, and even his favorite—onions. The old wolf couldn't believe his eyes.

Then he saw the goat happily eating the last few weeds. She saw him too, and froze in fear.

"You ate my weeds!" the old wolf said. "But why didn't you eat the vegetables?"

"Sorry, I'm a picky eater," she said. "Please don't eat me!"

The wolf looked at the plump goat and then at all the juicy vegetables, and back at the goat again. He sighed.

"Don't be sorry! You did my work for me. What's one breakfast compared to **delicious** vegetables for the rest of my days?"

The wolf smiled as he untied the goat.

"I could use a friend like you."

Plus, double-goat dumplings are overrated, anyway!

About the Author and Illustrator

John Rocco grew up in a small town in Rhode Island. He studied illustration at special art schools. He made illustrations for movies, theme parks, and museums. Now he makes children's books by writing stories and illustrating them. John and his family share a farmhouse with a family of mice, six bats, and some chipmunks.

Author's Purpose

Sometimes authors write to entertain their readers. Making characters say or do something surprising can be funny. What is something surprising the wolf says or does?

Respond to the Text

Summarize

Use important details about the characters, setting, and plot to summarize the story. Information from your Problem and Solution chart may help you.

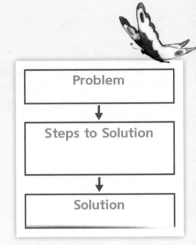

Problem

↓

Steps to Solution

↓

Solution

Write

How does the wolf change from the beginning of the story to the end? Use these sentence frames:

At the beginning of the story, the wolf . . .
When the wolf sees the goat eating his weeds, he feels . . .

Make Connections

What did the animals in this story teach you?
ESSENTIAL QUESTION

Why is it sometimes important to change your mind about something? **TEXT TO WORLD**

Compare Texts

Read stories from different cultures about Cinderella and her friends.

Cinderella and Friends

Cinderella is a lonely girl with only mice for friends. Then her animal friends help her get to a ball and everything changes. The traditional Cinderella story is from Europe, but there are Cinderella **stories** from around the world. People in different places tell different Cinderella stories. Read some of these stories, and see how Cinderella's animal friends help.

Illustration: Alex Steele-Morgan

Yeh-Shen, A Chinese Cinderella

Yeh-Shen's only friend is a beautiful fish. One day her fish died. Yeh-Shen buried its bones. The fish bones were magical so Yeh-Shen made a wish. She wanted to go to the spring festival. The fish bones gave her a beautiful dress and golden slippers to wear. At the festival, Yeh-Shen lost one of the slippers. The king found the lost slipper. He said that he wanted to marry its owner. Many girls tried on the golden slipper. It only fit Yeh-Shen. She married the king, and they lived happily ever after.

Rhodopis, An Egyptian Cinderella

Rhodopis was a poor servant girl. The other servants teased her. Her only friends were the animals along the river. She liked to sing and dance for them. They loved Rhodopis. One evening Rhodopis lost a slipper. A bird snatched it away. Then the bird flew over the king's castle. The slipper dropped onto his throne. The king searched his whole kingdom to find the girl whose foot fit the slipper. When he found Rhodopis, they fell in love and she became the queen.

A Zuni Cinderella Story

Some Native American stories have the same events as the Cinderella story. In one Zuni tale, a girl wanted to go to the sacred dance. But she did not have a dress to wear. Her only friends were the talking turkeys that she cared for. The turkeys took pity on the girl. They created a gown with feathers for her to wear. Then she could dance.

No matter where they come from, Cinderella stories teach similar **lessons**. The moral is that kindness will be rewarded. Hard beginnings can still have happy endings. It helps to have animal friends!

Make Connections

What can animals in stories teach you? ESSENTIAL QUESTION

Think about the animals in stories you have read this week. Which animals help others? Which play tricks? TEXT TO TEXT

Turtle, Turtle, Watch Out!

By **April Pulley Sayre**

Illustrated by **Annie Patterson**

Essential Question

What are features of different animal habitats?

Read about sea turtles that live in the ocean.

Go Digital!

Late one night, on a beach in Florida, a baby turtle's story begins. It could be a short story—or no story at all—if not for helping hands.

Turtle is only an egg now. Her mother's flippers cover her with sand.

Hungry raccoons watch. And when Mother Turtle crawls back to sea . . .

Furry feet scurry. Noses sniff. Paws dig.

Turtle, Turtle, watch out!

Young hands, holding a flashlight, scare the bandits away.

They place wire mesh around the turtle nest to protect the **buried** eggs.

Morning comes. So does a car. It speeds toward the eggs.

Turtle, Turtle, watch out!

The car stops. Hands have put up a painted sign.
NO DRIVING ON THE BEACH, the sign says.
The car leaves. The turtle nest is safe and undisturbed.
Turtle sees none of this, inside her egg.

Two months later, Turtle begins to tear her leathery eggshell. She rips it open with a special tooth. She rocks and wiggles to escape. Then she rests, still half in her shell. Her yolk sac, attached to the bottom of her shell, shrinks as her body absorbs its energy.

A day later, nudging and pushing, she and the other hatchlings dig toward the surface. They scramble, then rest. Scramble, then rest. Their upward journey takes three whole days.

Finally, on a moonlit August night, Turtle **peeks** out of the sand. Other hatchlings below her are pushing her upward. All around her, the hatchlings dig out.

Pushing against the sand, Turtle crawls across the beach. Go to the light! That's all Turtle knows. At night the brightest light should be the horizon over the sea.

Tonight it is not. Turtle crawls toward the wrong light, shining from across the street.

Turtle, Turtle, watch out!

STOP AND CHECK

Make Predictions Where do you think Turtle will crawl to? Make a prediction about what will happen.

Small hands switch off the light. Turtle turns and crawls the other way. She scurries toward the ocean waves.

Step by step, she **journeys** down the beach. Animals gather: night herons, cats, and raccoons. They are hungry and are here to eat the hatchlings.

Turtle, Turtle, watch out!

Quickly, Turtle scoots to the water. *Whoosh!* Water picks her up and carries her seaward, then pushes her back toward the beach. *Whoosh!* Waves tumble her tiny body, then carry her to sea again. She pushes her flippers. She can swim! She swims past hungry fish. Currents catch her and carry her far from shore.

For months, she drifts in patches of seaweed. She dines on tiny plants and animals. She grows. Currents carry her thousands of miles, circling an ocean wide, until one day she leaves the floating sargassum, a mass of algae. She begins to swim. Past islands. Past sailfish. Past humpback whales.

She reaches a coral reef, where she **spies** a tasty jellyfish. . . .

Turtle, Turtle, watch out!

Splash! Quick hands dip down, grabbing the plastic bag. It looks like a jellyfish, but it is not. It could choke a turtle or clog its belly.

Turtle swims onward. She looks for other food. As she grows, her jaws crack open conchs, crabs, and clams. For twenty years this is her turtle life . . . until one day she feels **restless**.

It is time for her to travel, far and fast. She flaps her flippers like underwater wings. She swims and swims—past ships, sailing and sunken.

Three sharks see her.

Turtle, Turtle, watch out!

STOP AND CHECK

Make Predictions What do you think will happen with the sharks? Make a prediction about what will happen.

The sharks pursue her. No hands can help her now. She swims faster and faster—and finally **escapes**! But she does not see a shrimper's nets rushing toward her.

Turtle, Turtle, watch out!

In an instant she is swept into a net. It drags her down, down. She needs to surface to breathe. The boat pulls, tumbling her to the back of the net. She is almost out of air—when she slips through an escape hatch. She is free!

Months before, weathered hands had sewn that hatch onto the net, just so sea turtles could escape.

Shaken but safe, Turtle swims on. She meets a male turtle, and they mate. Later, under a summer moon, Turtle swims toward the breaking waves.

Thud! Her heavy body hits the hard shore. It is the same beach where she hatched. But now things are different: now she is a mother turtle, about to lay her eggs.

One day those eggs will hatch. The tiny turtles will begin their journeys, scrambling across the sand. And some will make it, with a little luck, and fast-moving flippers, and the help of many hands.

About the Author and Illustrator

April Pulley Sayre has always loved science and writing. As a child she liked to watch birds, flowers, and insects. Now she writes books about snails, crabs, bumblebees, desert toads, whales, birds, and many other creatures. April has even written about dust!

Annie Patterson illustrates children's books. She enjoys watching the ocean and animals where she lives. Polar bears and snowy owls are some animals Annie sees by her home!

Author's Purpose

When authors repeat words in their writing, we call it *repetition*. Authors use repetition for a purpose. Why does April repeat the sentence "Turtle, Turtle, watch out!"?

Respond to the Text

Summarize

Use important details from the beginning, middle, and end to summarize the selection. Information from your Main Topic and Key Details chart may help you.

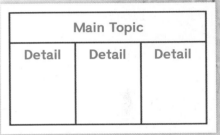

Main Topic		
Detail	Detail	Detail

Write

Starting at the beginning of the selection on page 166, the author uses the word *hands* repeatedly. What does this help us to understand? Use this sentence frame:

The word *hands* refers to…
The hands affect the turtle by…

Make Connections

What are the features of the ocean habitat where turtles live? **ESSENTIAL QUESTION**

What is something you learned about how people can help turtles to survive? **TEXT TO WORLD**

At Home in the River

Many animals call the *Cuyahoga River* home. It is a fresh-water **habitat**. Ocean water has salt, but the river does not. The Cuyahoga gives many animals shelter and food.

Food from the River

A family of wood ducks floats by. The mother leads her ducklings along the river bank. They eat plants that grow in the water. The plants are called duckweed.

Wood
Duck

CUYAHOGA RIVER HABITAT	
ANIMAL	**FOOD**
Wood Duck	duckweed, seeds, fruit
Spotted Turtle	snails, worms, spiders
Raccoon	fish, frogs, eggs, mice, insects

(bkgd) Jason Langley/age fotostock (inset) Paul E. Tessier/Photodisc/Getty Images

A Spotted Turtle's Journey

Spotted turtles sun themselves on a floating log. They have dots on their heads and shells. One turtle leaves the river to lay eggs. On the river bank, she stops to eat snails and worms.

When she finds a place, she digs a hole with her back legs. She covers her eggs with dirt to hide them from other animals. A raccoon sleeps in a hole in the tree. It would enjoy this meal. After two months, the baby turtles hatch. They journey to the river bank.

Every living thing is important in **nature.** Each living thing needs and helps another. Each plant and animal lives and then begins a new cycle. Life in the river keeps going.

Spotted Turtle

Raccoon

Make Connections

What are the features of this river habitat? **ESSENTIAL QUESTION**

Think about the different habitats you read about this week. What do they all provide for animals? **TEXT TO TEXT**

Baby Bears

by
Bobbie Kalman

Essential Question

How are offspring like their parents?

Read to find out how baby bears are like their moms and dads.

Go Digital!

What is a bear?

Bears are animals called **mammals**. Mammals have hair or **fur** on their bodies. Bears are **covered** with fur. Mammals are born. You were born, too. You are a mammal.

Baby bears are called cubs. Cubs are born with their eyes shut. Their eyes open when they are about six weeks old. This brown bear cub was just born. It has very little fur.

Mammal mothers make milk inside their bodies. Mammal babies nurse from their mothers. To nurse is to drink mother's milk.

The polar bear cub is nursing.

Kinds of bears

There are eight kinds of bears. The bears shown on this page are an American black bear, a brown bear, and a polar bear. These bears all live in North America.

American black bears can be different colors. What color is this black bear?

There are different kinds of brown bears. These grizzly bears are one kind of brown bear.

Polar bears have white fur. They live in a cold place called the Arctic.

(t) Anthony Cassidy/Photographer's Choice/Getty Images (c) Richard Seeley/iStock/360/Getty Images (b) Theo Allofs/Digital Vision/Getty Images

People who study bears once thought that **giant** pandas were raccoons. Now people think that these animals are bears. There are not many giant pandas left in the world. Giant pandas live in China.

STOP AND CHECK

Reread What animal did people used to think giant pandas were? Reread to check your understanding.

Bear bodies

Bears have four legs. They can walk on all four legs or on their two back legs. They have five toes with claws on each foot. Claws are curved nails.

This grizzly bear cub has brown fur covering its body.

Bears can smell, hear, and see very well.

Bears use their claws to climb and dig.

Bear coats

Bears have two kinds of fur. Some of their fur is short, and some is long. Their short fur keeps them warm. Their long fur keeps water away from their skin.

Polar bears have thick white fur.

Pandas have black-and-white fur.

A bear family is made up of a mother bear and her cubs. Most mother bears have litters of cubs. A litter is two or more babies that are born at the same time. This mother grizzly bear has three cubs.

This mother bear is teaching her cubs how to climb a tree. Mothers also teach cubs how to **groom** their fur and stay clean.

Cubs stay with their mothers until they are two to three years old. They watch their mothers to learn how to live on their own. Mother bears teach their cubs where to find food and how to stay safe.

What do bears eat?

Most bears are omnivores. Omnivores are animals that eat both plants and animals. Bears eat honey, berries, leaves, and eggs. They also eat insects, fish, and other animals. Polar bears are carnivores. Carnivores eat mainly other animals. Pandas are herbivores. Herbivores eat mainly plants.

Pandas eat plants called bamboo.

Bear habitats

Bears live in different places. The natural place where a bear lives is called its habitat. Many bears live in forests. Forests are habitats with many trees. Some bears live on mountains. Pandas live in forests that grow high on mountains. Bamboo grows in these forests.

Black bears live in North American forests.

STOP AND CHECK

Make Predictions What do you think this bear will find to eat? Use the Make Predictions strategy to help you.

Winter sleep

Some bears live in places that have cold winters. It is hard for the bears to find food when it is cold. To stay **alive**, they sleep through most of the winter. During the summer and fall, the bears eat a lot of food. They store the food as fat on their bodies. The bears live off the fat during the winter.

These grizzly bears are eating a lot of salmon. They are getting ready for winter.

Mother bears that live in cold places have their cubs in winter. Before the cubs are born, the mother builds a home called a den. The den is a warm and safe place for the bears to live. Many bears make their dens by digging holes in hills or under tree roots. Some bears use caves or holes in logs for their dens. After the cubs are born, the mother goes to sleep. The cubs nurse while their mother sleeps.

Some polar bears make tunnels in the snow to use as dens.

Cubs grow up

Each bear goes through a set of changes called a life cycle. A life cycle starts when a cub is born. The cub grows and changes. It then becomes an **adult** bear. These pictures show the life cycle of an American black bear.

Adult bears can make babies.

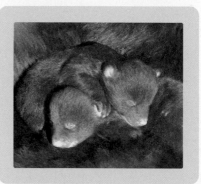

The cub becomes an adult when it is three to five years old.

A black bear cub drinks its mother's milk.

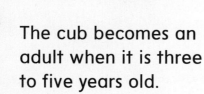

Soon the cub leaves the den. It still nurses, but it starts eating other foods too.

This mother bear and her cubs are looking for food in a forest. The cubs will soon start living on their own and finding food for themselves.

This black bear cub has just left its den. It is starting to learn about the world. The cub will quickly find out why it should not play with skunks!

About the Author

Bobbie Kalman has written books about almost every kind of animal. Once she spent months in Hawaii swimming with dolphins and whales so she could write about them. *Baby Bears* is Bobbie's first book about baby animals. She loves writing about how they learn, grow, and change.

Author's Purpose

Authors often use headings in expository text. What are some of the headings in *Baby Bears*? How do these headings help you understand the information?

Respond to the Text

Summarize

Use important details to summarize the selection. Information from your Main Topic and Key Details chart may help you.

Main Topic		
Detail	Detail	Detail

Write

How does the way the author organized information help you understand how bears grow? Use these sentence frames:

The author starts with a bear....
Then the author organizes the information by...

Make Connections

How do baby bears learn from their mothers?
ESSENTIAL QUESTION

What can people learn about babies and parents from studying bears? **TEXT TO WORLD**

Compare Texts
Read about how baby caterpillars become butterflies.

From Caterpillar to Butterfly

A butterfly is not a **mammal**. It does not have live babies or feed milk to its young. A butterfly is an insect. It lays eggs.

Look at the photo. Can you tell which is the parent and which is the **offspring**? Probably not! The parent is the butterfly, and its baby is the caterpillar. The parent and the offspring do not look alike right now. However, when the caterpillar is grown, it will look like its parent.

Butterfly Life Cycle

1. Egg
The adult butterfly lays an egg on a milkweed leaf.

2. Larva
After 3 or 4 days, a tiny caterpillar comes out of the egg. Caterpillars are a kind of larva. The caterpillar eats its shell for food.

3. Caterpillar
For about two weeks, the caterpillar eats leaves and grows bigger.

4. Chrysalis
The caterpillar forms a shell around itself. The shell is called a chrysalis.

5. Adult

Two weeks later, an adult butterfly comes out of the chrysalis. It will lay an egg on a leaf, and the cycle will continue.

Make Connections
How is a caterpillar like its parents?
ESSENTIAL QUESTION

How is a butterfly's offspring different from a bear cub? **TEXT TO TEXT**

(tl) Ingram Publishing/Alamy (tc) Ed Reschke/Photolibrary/Getty Images (tr) Don Johnston/Alamy (bl) Don Johnston IH/Alamy Stock Photo (br) Eric Bean/Digital Vision/Getty Images

"Beetles", from GOOSE-GRASS RHYMES by Monica Shannon, copyright 1930 by Doubleday, a division of Random House, Inc. Used by permission of Doubleday, a division of Random House, Inc.

Essential Question

What do we love about animals?

Read poems that **express** what we love about animals.

Go Digital!

Beetles

by Monica Shannon

Beetles must use polish,
   They look so new and shiny,
Just like a freshly painted car,
   Except for being tiny.

Illustration: Steven Mach

The Little Turtle

by Vachel Lindsay

There was a little turtle.
He lived in a box.
He swam in a puddle.
He climbed on the rocks.

He snapped at a mosquito.
He snapped at a flea.
He snapped at a minnow.
And he snapped at me.

He caught the mosquito.
He caught the flea.
He caught the minnow.
But he didn't catch me.

Respond to the Text

Summarize

Use important details from "The Little Turtle" to describe the poem. Information from your Key Details chart may help you.

Detail	Detail	Detail

Write

What about these creatures inspires the poets to write about them? How do they show it? Use these sentence frames:

Beetles are like freshly painted cars because . . .
The poet repeats . . .

Make Connections

What do you love about animals? ESSENTIAL QUESTION

Each poem describes the way an animal **behaves**. What are some ways animals you have seen look and act? TEXT TO WORLD

Genre • Poetry

Compare Texts
Read about a mother goose and her baby.

Gray Goose

by Julie Larios

Gray mama goose
in a tizzy,
honk-honk-honking herself dizzy,
can't find her gosling,
she's honking and running,
webbed feet slapping,
all wild waddle,
her **feathers** a muddle,
splashing through puddles,
wings **flapping**. . . .

Ah,
there's her gold baby,
all fuzz,
napping.

Make Connections

What do you love about this goose and her baby? ESSENTIAL QUESTION

What did the poems you have read this week **express** about how animals **behave**? TEXT TO TEXT

211

I Fall Down

By Vicki Cobb
Illustrated by Julia Gorton

Essential Question

How do the Earth's forces affect us?

Read about how gravity pushes and pulls.

Go Digital!

Know what happens
when you trip?

You fall down!

Know what happens
when you spill your milk?

It drips down!

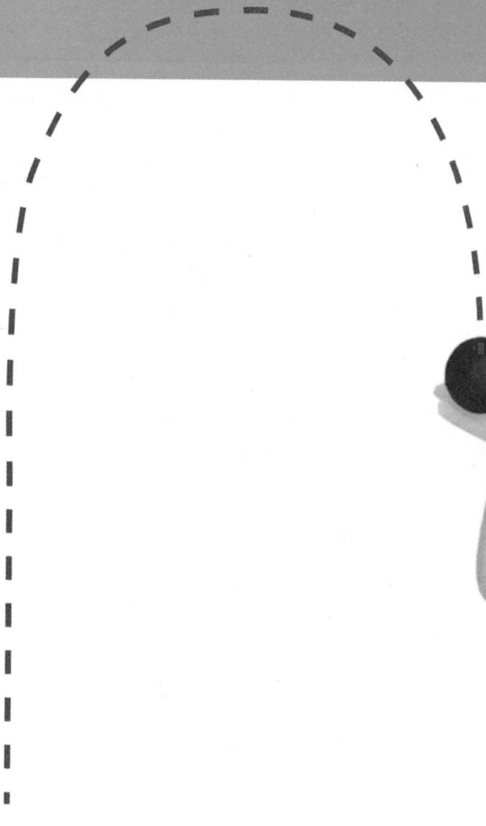

Throw a ball up into
the air. Watch what
happens. It goes up
for a short time, then
falls down.

Try tossing other things up in the air.

Your mom's keys.

A block.

When something falls, which way does it fall?

Does it ever fall up?

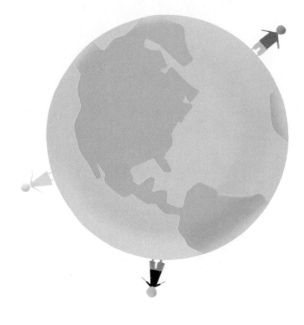

It's a **force** called gravity. As long as you are on Earth, you can't get away from it.

Gravity is always pulling things.

Know which way?

Down, down, down.

You can see how gravity pulls.

Take a spoonful of molasses or honey and point the spoon down so that the goo dribbles back into the jar.

Watch it drip!

The goo stretches and gets longer and longer. It looks like a ribbon streaming into the jar. Gravity pulls the molasses from the spoon back into the jar.

Do some things fall faster than others?

Try it and see!

Hold a penny and a key in one hand. Open your hand so they both start falling at the same time. Listen and watch as they hit the floor.

Did either the penny or the key win the race, or was it a tie?

Things fall so fast it's hard to tell if there is a winner or a loser.

Have lots of dropping races.

But no matter whether the **objects** are big or small, it seems that it's always a tie.

The only time you have a clear loser is when you drop something that the wind could easily blow away, such as a feather or a tissue. You see air fighting gravity only with very light objects.

STOP AND CHECK

Reread Why are the dropping races always a tie? Reread to check your understanding.

If there were no air, you would find that gravity pulls everything at the same speed.

Astronauts proved this on the moon, where there is no air.

Every dropping race was a tie.

AMAZING BUT TRUE!

Does everything land with the same force? Or do some things hit harder than others?

Here's a way to find out.

Have someone drop a dry sponge into your hand from about a foot above it. Next try a small bar of soap. Which hits your hand harder, the sponge or the soap?

Try dropping lots of things into your hand.

Soon you will discover that some things hit harder than others.

Now hold the bar of soap in one hand

and the sponge in the other.

Which is heavier, the sponge or the soap?

Move your hands **up** and **down** to feel the difference.

Your hands stop the sponge and the soap from falling to the ground.

But you can still feel gravity's pull on the soap and sponge when you hold them in your hands. This pull is called **weight**.

STOP AND CHECK

Reread What is weight? Reread to check your understanding.

223

You can see if one object is heavier than another without letting either of them fall.

Here's how.

Get two rubber bands the same size.

Tie one of your shoes to one rubber band. Tie one of your parent's shoes to the other rubber band.

Which rubber band stretches more?

The heavier shoe stretches
the rubber band more.
Each rubber band acts like
a scale to **measure** weight.

Your weight is a measure of how hard you fall when you fall down.

How much do you weigh?

How much does your mother or father weigh?

98

85

167

50

48

91

225

The more you weigh, the harder you fall.

But you don't have to fall in order to weigh yourself.

A scale tells you how hard you fall—

without you falling at all!

So simply get on a scale.

Yay!

About the Author and Illustrator

Vicki Cobb likes to test out gravity on the ski slopes. Gravity pulls her one way on the hill—down! Vicki loved the creative tasks and hands-on experiments she did at her New York City elementary school. They made science fun. Vicki loved learning that way so much that today she writes books to help other kids learn the same way.

Julia Gorton sees gravity in action every day—while she watches her three children skateboard. Julia illustrates books and teaches at an art school.

Author's Purpose

Vicki asks the reader questions throughout *I Fall Down*. What do you think her purpose is for asking questions?

Respond to the Text

Summarize

Use important details to summarize the selection. Information from your Author's Purpose chart may help you.

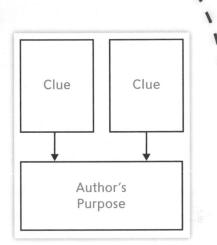

Write

How does the author show how gravity and weight are related through illustrations? Use these sentence frames:

The text placement adds to the illustrations by...
The illustrations of the soap and the sponge...

Make Connections

How does the force of gravity affect us?
ESSENTIAL QUESTION

What is something you learned about gravity from *I Fall Down* that surprised you?
TEXT TO WORLD

Move It!

All About Motion

Look for pushes and pulls that cause motion on the playground.

Position is the place where something is. When something moves, it changes its position. A change in position is called motion. But what causes motion?

Think about a swing. Like other objects, a swing cannot move by itself. It needs the push or pull of a different **force**. A person can push a swing. He or she can also pull it. Pushes and pulls keep a swing moving in a back-and-forth motion.

Stockbyte/PunchStock

Motion in Action

Where can you see lots of motion? A soccer game! Many forces are at play in a game. Each kick is a push that moves the ball. If a player kicks hard, the ball moves at a fast **speed**. However, if the player gives the ball a gentle tap, it moves slowly. Speed is how far something moves in a certain amount of time.

A player might kick the ball in a straight line. He or she can kick the ball up in the air, but the force of gravity will bring it back down. Kicking the ball in a zigzag path gets it away from players. The goalie can pull the ball away. Until the game is over, the motion never stops.

Force		
	Push	Pull
	X	
		X
	X	

Make Connections

How do the forces of pushes and pulls affect objects? ESSENTIAL QUESTION

What have you read about the force of gravity this week? TEXT TO TEXT

Genre · Fiction

Essential Question
What can we see in the sky?

Read about what Mr. Putter and Tabby see in the **nighttime** sky.

Go Digital!

232

Mr. Putter & Tabby See the Stars

by Cynthia Rylant

illustrated by Arthur Howard

Chapter 1

Logs

Mr. Putter and his fine cat, Tabby, loved
to sleep.
They could sleep anywhere.
They slept in chairs, in swings, in cars, in
tubs, and sometimes in the laundry room.

Mr. Putter and Tabby also slept in
a bed. Of course, most of the time,
sleeping in a bed was just fine.
Mr. Putter plumped his pillow. Tabby
squished hers. And then they slept like logs.

But one night, one of the logs could not sleep.

Chapter 2

Grumble

Mr. Putter was the log who could not sleep.
He could not sleep because he had
eaten too many pineapple jelly rolls at
Mrs. Teaberry's house.

Mrs. Teaberry was Mr. Putter's good friend
and **neighbor**, and she liked to feed him.
She liked to feed everybody.
But most of all, she liked
to feed Mr. Putter.

She was always sending her good dog, Zeke,
over to Mr. Putter's house with a note.
The note always said, "Are you hungry?"
And Mr. Putter always said, "Yes."
So he and Tabby went next door a lot.

But tonight Mr. Putter had been having
such a good time that he lost track and ate
twenty-one jelly rolls.
He forgot to count them as he popped them
one at a time into his mouth.

Before he knew it, twenty-one jelly rolls
were gone, and it was time to go home.

Mrs. Teaberry was happy that Mr. Putter **enjoyed** her jelly rolls so much.
But Mr. Putter's stomach was not.
It **grumbled** and grumbled and grumbled.

Mr. Putter looked at his nice soft bed when he got home.
G-R-U-M-B-L-E grumbled his stomach.
Mr. Putter knew he would not be able to sleep with all that grumbling.
What to do?
Mr. Putter looked at Tabby.
Then he got an idea.

Chapter 3

Stars

"Let's go for a walk," Mr. Putter said.

He put his coat back on.

He put his hat back on.

He picked up Tabby.

And out the door they went.

It was a beautiful night.

The moon was full, and
moonlight was everywhere.

Tabby looked. She listened.
She twitched her ears.
She twitched her tail.
She loved the night.
Mr. Putter loved it, too, even
with a grumbling stomach.

STOP AND CHECK

Reread Why is Mr. Putter's
stomach grumbling? Reread
to check your understanding.

241

Mr. Putter looked up at the sky.
He showed Tabby the stars, and he
told her all about them.
He told her that the Big Dipper was
full of milk from the Milky Way.
Tabby purred. She loved milk.

He told her about looking
at stars when he was a boy.
And how he had always wanted
to ride in a rocket ship.
He told her how he had always
dreamed of **adventure**.

Tabby purred some more.
Mr. Putter and Tabby made
a nice big circle around
the neighborhood.

They looked at the sky.
They looked at the yellow lights of the houses.

They looked at cats sitting in windows,
looking back at them.

And when at last they circled back home,
they stopped in front of Mrs. Teaberry's house.
Mrs. Teaberry and Zeke were on the front lawn!
"Mrs. Teaberry, what are you doing up?"
asked Mr. Putter.

STOP AND CHECK

Reread Mr. Putter asks why Mrs. Teaberry is up. Why is Mr. Putter up, too? Reread to check your understanding.

245

"Zeke has a grumbling stomach," said
Mrs. Teaberry.
"He ate too many jelly rolls and we can't sleep."

Mr. Putter and Tabby were **delighted**.
They sat on the lawn with Mrs. Teaberry and Zeke.

Mr. Putter's stomach and Zeke's stomach
talked to each other while Mr. Putter
and Mrs. Teaberry talked to each other.

They told stories in the moonlight.
They told secrets.
They made each other laugh.

Then when the stomachs on the front lawn stopped grumbling, everyone said good night, went to bed, and slept like logs.

There's no place like home.

There's no business like show business.

In the morning, Mr. Putter heard a
scratching at the door.
He opened it.

It was Zeke with a note.
The note said, "Are you hungry?"

Mr. Putter smiled.
He picked up Tabby and together they
walked next door.

About the Author and Illustrator

Cynthia Rylant was a teacher and a librarian before she became a writer. She began reading children's books while working at a library. That's when she decided she wanted to make her own. When she gets an idea, she says, "I sit down with pen and paper, and soon I've got a story going!"

Arthur Howard used to be an actor in plays and on television. Now he writes and illustrates books for children. When he started the Mr. Putter & Tabby series, Arthur drew Mr. Putter to look like his own father. Tabby is based on his mother's cat, Red.

Author's Purpose

Cynthia divides *Mr. Putter & Tabby See the Stars* into chapters. Why do you think she uses the chapter names "Logs," "Grumbles," and "Stars"?

Respond to the Text

Summarize

Use important details to summarize what happens in the story. Information from your Sequence chart may help you.

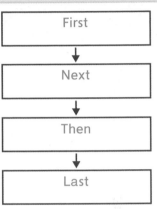

Write

How does the author show the connection between Mr. Putter and Mrs. Teaberry? Use these sentence frames:

The author says that Mr. Putter...
This shows a connection to Mrs. Teaberry because...

Make Connections

What do Mr. Putter and Tabby see in the sky?
ESSENTIAL QUESTION

Tell about something that you can see or have learned about the nighttime sky. **TEXT TO WORLD**

Day to Night

Your alarm clock rings. *Beep! Beep! Beep!* You turn it off, stretch, and get out of bed. You look out the window and see the daytime sky.

The Daytime Sky

The sky is light today. It is blue with white clouds and the bright Sun. The Sun is the brightest object in the sky. It looks small, but that is because it is far from Earth.

Sometimes the daytime sky has clouds.

The Sun

The Sun is actually a star. Like all stars, it is a huge ball of hot gases. The Sun is much larger than the Earth. It is the Earth's closest star, but there are many stars in the sky. In fact, there are too many stars in the sky to count! We cannot see them during the day because the Sun's light makes our sky too bright.

Hello, Sun . . . Goodbye, Sun

If you watched the Sun all day, it would look like it moves across the sky. But the Sun does not move. Even though you cannot feel it, Earth is turning. It makes one full turn in 24 hours, or one day. For about half of those hours, the place where you live faces the Sun. It is daytime. The rest of the time, your home is not facing the Sun. Then it is dark.

When the Sun is shining on your home, it is daytime. Then the Earth turns. When your home faces away from the Sun, it is nighttime.

(t) Design Pics/Kristy-Anne Glubish (b) NASA/NOAA/SPL/Science Photo Library/Getty Images

The stars look like tiny points of light, but each one is very big.

The Nighttime Sky

At the end of the day, you look out the window before you get into bed. The sky is dark. It is **nighttime**. Tonight you see part of the moon. Without the bright light from the Sun, you are able to see light from many stars.

The Moon

The Moon is a large ball made of rock. As Earth spins, the Moon turns around Earth. It takes about one month for the Moon to go around Earth one time. The Sun's light shines on the Moon. As the Moon moves during a month, the amount of sunlight shining on the Moon at night changes. This changes how we see the Moon. We see **moonlight** because the Sun's light shines on the Moon.

Phases of the Moon

We see a Full Moon about once a month.

Make Connections

? What can you see in the daytime and nighttime sky? ESSENTIAL QUESTION

What do people like to look for or watch in the sky? TEXT TO TEXT

Genre • Narrative Nonfiction

BIBLIOBURRO

A True Story From Colombia

Jeanette Winter

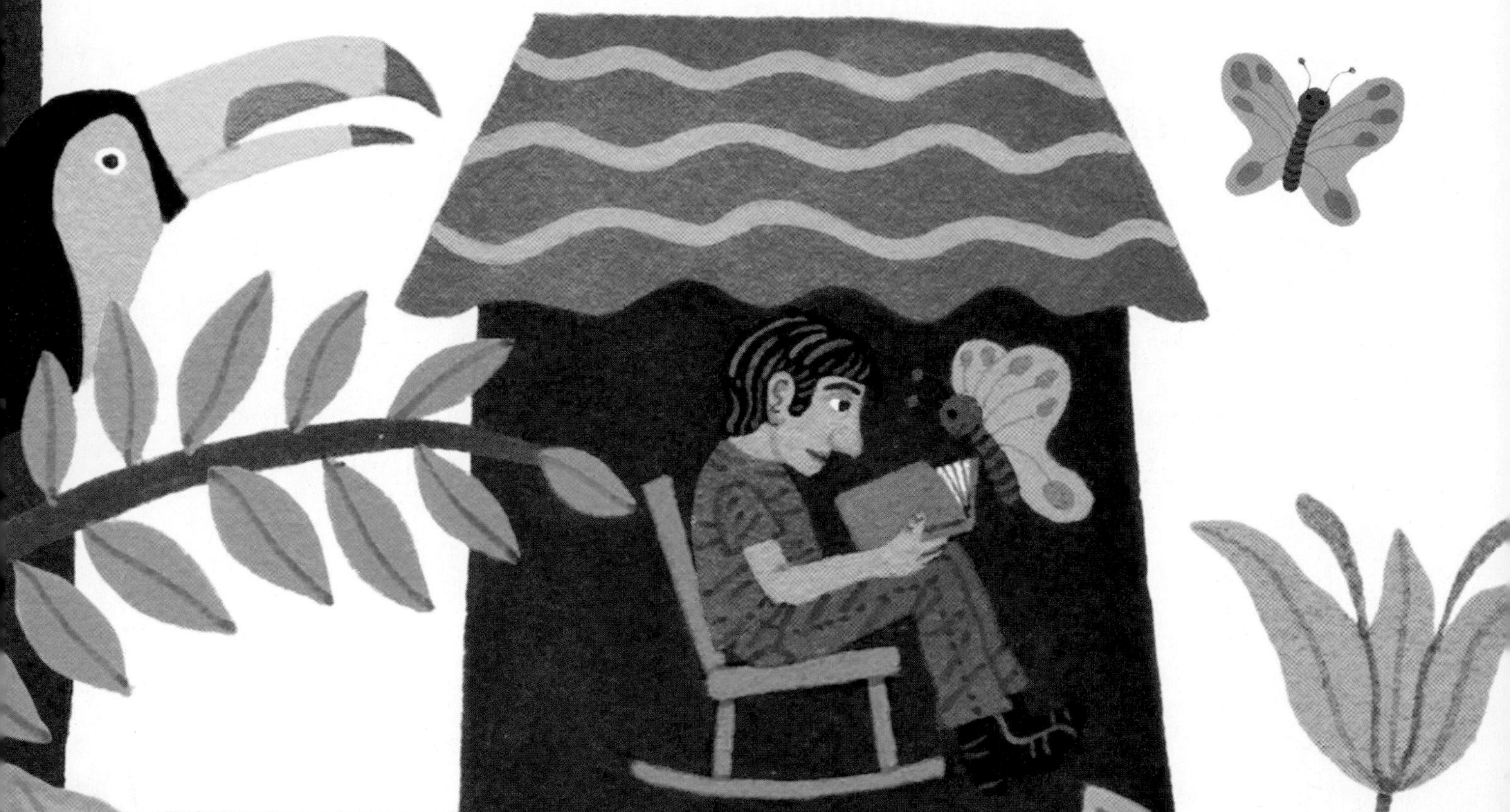

Essential Question

How can people help out in their community?

Read about a man who travels to bring books to faraway villages that have none.

Go Digital!

Deep in the jungles of Colombia, there lives a man who loves books.

His name is Luis.

As soon as he reads one book, he brings home another. Soon the house is filled with books.

His wife, Diana, grumbles.

What are we going to do, eat books with our rice?

Luis thinks long and hard.

At last an **idea** pops into his head.

"I can bring my books into the faraway hills to share with those who have none.

One burro could carry books, and another burro could carry me—and more books!"

Luis buys two sturdy little burros.

He names them Alfa and Beto.

He builds crates to hang on their backs,
and paints signs: BIBLIOBURRO—
"The Burro Library."

Then Diana fills the crates with books.

Every week, Luis and Alfa and Beto set off **across** the **countryside** to faraway **villages** in the **lonely** hills.

This week they travel to El Tormento.

STOP AND CHECK

Ask and Answer Questions
Why are Luis, Alfa, and Beto going to El Tormento? Go back to the text to find the answer.

263

When the sun burns high in the sky,
Luis and the burros stop at a stream
to drink the cool water.

After they have their fill,
Beto balks.

BIBLIO BURRO

Luis pulls and pulls on Beto's reins,
but Beto won't budge.

The children are waiting for us!

At last the burro gives in
and steps across the stream.

The Biblioburro continues on its way
over the hills, until at last,
Luis sees houses below.

The children of El Tormento run to meet him.

Luis **insists** on reading a story
before they choose books to **borrow**.

"Today I have a surprise for you," he says.

He reaches behind the books
and pulls out a bundle of masks—little piglets!

"Put on a mask, and I'll read you a tale
about pigs."

269

When the story ends,
it's time for everyone
to choose a book.

The children hold their books close
as they say good-bye and walk home.

Luis and Alfa and Beto head back,
over and around the hills,

across the grasslands and streams,
and into the sunset.

STOP AND CHECK

Reread Where are Luis, Alfa, and Beto going now? Reread to check your understanding.

273

But then, instead of sleeping,
Luis picks up *his* book,
and reads deep into the night.

And far away in the hills,
candles and lanterns burn
as the children read borrowed books
deep into *their* night, too.

275

About the Author and Illustrator

Jeanette Winter loved to write stories and draw pictures as a child. She wanted to be an artist when she grew up. Jeanette studied painting, drawing, and sculpture. She taught herself about illustrating books. As an adult Jeanette has won many awards for her books.

Jeanette likes to write stories about real people. She often finds her ideas while she is reading the newspaper. *Biblioburro* tells the true story of Luis Soriano, a schoolteacher in Colombia. When Luis started sharing books with villages, he had 70 to share. Now he has over 4,800 books to loan!

Author's Purpose

Why do you think Jeanette tells Luis's story? What do you think her purpose is?

276

Respond to the Text

Summarize

Use important details to summarize what happens in the selection. Information from your Author's Purpose chart may help you.

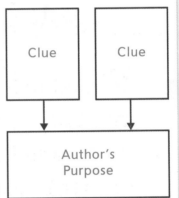

Write

How does the author use illustrations to show the difficulty of Luis's journey? Use these sentence starters:

The author showed Luis thinking about his journey by . . .

There are images of the burros carrying . . .

Make Connections

How did Luis help out in his community?
ESSENTIAL QUESTION

What is something you learned about reading or libraries from *Biblioburro*?
TEXT TO WORLD

The Enormous Turnip

One night a farmer went out in his garden and planted turnip seeds. The next morning, the family looked out the window and saw a huge turnip growing in the garden. It was so big it blocked the sunlight. "We will have lots of turnip soup tonight!" cried the children.

The farmer hurried outside to harvest the turnip. He pulled and tugged, but the turnip would not come out of the ground.

The farmer's wife and children came to help. The family worked together, but the turnip still would not budge.

Illustration: Alison Jay

Other people in their village saw the family tugging at the turnip. "Let us help you!" they cried. "Many hands make light work."

The villagers had an **idea**. They held onto each other's waists to make a chain. Together, they all pulled at the turnip in the ground. Finally, the ground rumbled, and the turnip popped out!

The farmer chopped up the turnip and his wife got a big pot. "Turnip soup for all who helped!" he announced.

All the neighbors took a serving. "We all worked together to find a **solution** to the problem," said the farmer. "So now we all get a tasty meal as a reward."

Make Connections

How did the farmer and his family help out their community? ESSENTIAL QUESTION

Think about the other selections you've read this week. What are some other ways people help in their communities? TEXT TO TEXT

WILD WEATHER

By Seymour Simon

Essential Question

How does weather affect us?

Read about how stormy weather affects people and places.

Go Digital!

Air is all around us. The air moves and winds blow. Changes in the air are called **weather**.

Sometimes weather is sunny and fair. Other times it's cloudy and rainy. Storms are sudden, **harsh** changes in the weather.

Thunderstorms

A **thunderstorm** is a heavy rain shower. In a few minutes, a big thunderstorm can drop millions of gallons of water. Hundreds of thunderstorms pop up every second somewhere around the world. These storms have lightning. Thunder is the sound of lightning.

Lightning

Lightning is a giant spark of electricity. A bolt of lightning is six to ten miles long but only as thick as your finger. Lightning is hotter than the surface of the sun. A bolt of lightning can be very dangerous and cause harm. The heat of a lightning bolt can set fire to a tree or a house.

Would you like to know how far away the lightning you see is? Count the number of seconds between the lightning flash and the clap of thunder. Every five seconds equals one mile away. If thunder booms a second or two after you see lightning, that's a **warning**. The sound means that the lightning bolt is very close to you.

How Lightning Works

Cold Air Sinks

Hot Air Rises

Electrical charges build up between the ground and cloud.

Tornadoes

Thunderstorms sometimes give birth to a string of tornadoes, or twisters. Dark, twisting tornadoes reach downward from the storm. The winds in a tornado whirl hundreds of miles per hour. They can lift heavy trucks into the air. They can **destroy** houses by blowing away their roofs.

On May 22nd, 2011, a tornado a mile wide ripped through the city of Joplin, Missouri. The huge tornado hurt many people. It destroyed buildings and damaged most of the city.

The tornado damaged this house in Joplin, Missouri.

Watches and Warnings

An early warning on television, radio stations, and the Internet helps to save lives. An early alert is called a tornado **watch**. A tornado **warning** means that a tornado has been seen. A tornado warning means that you should find shelter.

STOP AND CHECK

Ask and Answer Questions
What does a tornado warning mean? Go back to the text to find the answer.

Hurricanes

Hurricanes are the biggest storms of all. They hurt more people and destroy more buildings than all other kinds of storms put together. Hurricanes happen during the summer and early fall. They form over warm ocean waters. Then they move and may reach land. Hurricanes stretch for hundreds of miles. Their dangerous winds blow at speeds between 74 and 200 miles per hour. Waves from the storms may wash away shorelines, boats, and houses.

STOP AND CHECK

Ask and Answer Questions When do hurricanes happen? Go back to the text to find the answer.

In August, 2005, Hurricane Katrina became one of the worst storms in history. Many people in Louisiana were left homeless because of Katrina. The **damage** to buildings in the city of New Orleans cost billions of dollars.

Rain from Hurricane Katrina flooded this street in New Orleans.

David Howells/Corbis Historical/Getty Images

Blizzards

Hurricanes are warm-weather storms. Blizzards are huge winter snowstorms. Two or three inches of snow fall every hour. Temperatures are below freezing. Strong winds blow fiercely.

In February, 2007, a Valentine's Day blizzard hit the eastern half of North America. Heavy snowfalls blanketed much of the country. Some places had up to four feet of snow. Millions of homes lost power for days. Thousands of people were stuck in airports and on snowy highways.

No one can **prevent** a storm. Stormy weather can happen anywhere. Someday you and your family may be in a big storm. If you know what to do in advance, you will be safer when the next storm strikes.

SAFETY TIPS

Here are some storm safety tips for you and your family.

- Stay inside during strong storms.
- Keep a storm safety kit with bottled water and flashlights handy.
- Stay away from windows.
- Stay away from downed power lines.

ABOUT THE AUTHOR

Seymour Simon has always been interested in science. When he was a teenager in New York City, he was president of the Junior Astronomy Club. He even built his own telescope to see the stars!

Seymour taught science to kids for many years before he became a writer. He hasn't given up teaching, though. "I never will, not as long as I keep writing and talking to kids around the country and the world." Seymour has written more than 250 books on science and has won many important awards. His books make science clear, easy to understand, and fun.

AUTHOR'S PURPOSE

What do you think was Seymour's purpose for writing *Wild Weather*?

Respond to the Text

Summarize

Use important details to summarize what you learned in the selection. Information from your Main Idea and Details chart will help you.

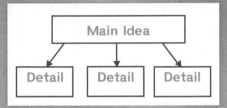

Write

How does the author help you understand how stormy weather can affect people? Use these sentence frames:

The author uses...
The photographs show...
Captions also tell me...

Make Connections

How does wild weather affect us? ESSENTIAL QUESTION

What are some things you learned about lightning from the selection? TEXT TO WORLD

Genre • Expository Text

Compare Texts
Read about tools people use
to predict the weather.

A wind vane has
an arrow. The wind
blows the arrow and
shows the direction
of the wind.

CAN YOU PREDICT THE WEATHER?

People want to know what the **weather** is like.
They want to know how hot or cold it is outside.
They want to know if it will rain or snow. They
need to know about a **dangerous** weather **event**,
such as a thunderstorm.

What Is the Weather Like Now?

Some tools tell people what the weather
is like. People can use these tools at home.
A *thermometer* tells the temperature. It
measures how hot or cold the air is. A
wind vane shows the wind's direction. The
wind vane spins and shows where the wind is
coming from. If the wind direction changes, the
weather will change, too.

The thermometer
has red liquid in
a tube. It moves
up when it is
hot outside.

The radar picture shows where big storms are. The red parts show severe weather.

How Do Scientists Predict the Weather?

Some tools tell what the weather is like right now, but other tools tell what the weather will be like in the future. *Meteorologists* are people who study weather. They use tools to predict the weather. Their predictions are called a forecast.

Meteorologists use radar, a tool that uses waves of energy to track the weather. A radar picture shows if rain, snow, or big storms are coming. Radar helps us stay safe. It gives a **warning** when a bad storm is coming. It shows the speed and direction a storm is moving.

Thunderstorm Safety

DO:
- Stay indoors.
- Stay away from hilltops and open fields if outdoors.
- Stay low if outside.

DON'T:
- Stand under a tree.
- Go in or near water.
- Stay on your bike.

Make Connections

How do tools help us understand how the weather affects us? ESSENTIAL QUESTION

What are some ways people can stay safe from dangerous weather? TEXT TO TEXT

Many Ways to Enjoy Music

Essential Question

How do you express yourself?

Read about how people express themselves through music.

Go Digital!

Rune Hellestad/Corbis Entertainment/Getty Images

How do deaf music lovers enjoy concerts?

At a **concert**, loud **music** booms from the stage. The band rocks their guitars and other **instruments**. Drums pound and clash. The fans clap and sing. Their ears are buzzing when the concert is over. However you don't need to listen up to enjoy a music concert. Many people who are unable to hear love going to concerts.

At this rock concert, a deaf fan sensed the excitement. She saw the band take the stage. She **cheered** by shaking her fist in the air. Her big smile showed that she really loved the concert!

A deaf fan and her son enjoy a concert. They sat in seats close to an interpreter.

STOP AND CHECK

Ask and Answer Questions What things will happen at a concert? Go back to the text to find the answer.

Making Music

At some concerts, rock bands perform. At others, orchestras play. An orchestra is a group of musicians playing instruments together. Most orchestras have four sections.

Here is a look at the number of instruments in each section.

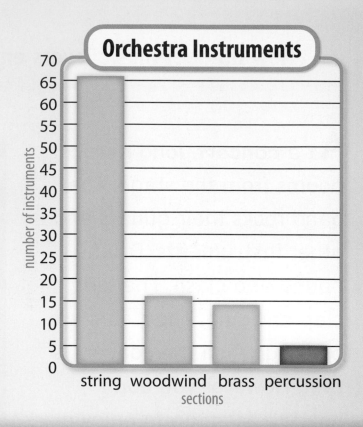

Orchestra Instruments

number of instruments

string   woodwind   brass   percussion
sections

An interpreter is a person who uses sign language to show the words of the song.

Kevin Winter/Getty Images Entertainment/Getty Images

Watching the Signs

One way deaf people enjoy a concert is by watching an interpreter. Interpreters use body **movements,** like swaying or jumping, to communicate what is happening on stage. By watching interpreters move, fans can **understand** what the band is singing.

Colin McConnell/Toronto Star/Getty Images

The movements help users feel what the music expresses. These chairs really rock!

Rock and Relax

Another way for deaf people to enjoy a concert is with technology. A special chair moves with the music's **rhythm**. A loud, pounding sound makes the chair beat hard. Deaf fans feel the rhythm on their backs. Low, quiet **sounds** makes the chair beat softer. The fans can feel the rhythm on the lower parts of their bodies.

Interpreters and technology are just some of the many ways deaf people can enjoy a concert.

Respond to the Text

Use details from the selection to summarize. SUMMARIZE

Is "Many Ways to Enjoy Music" a good title for this selection? Why or why not? WRITE

How can people express themselves through music? TEXT TO WORLD

Compare Texts
Read about a museum for
musical instruments and sounds.

courtesy of the Musical Instrument Museum

A Musical Museum

At a recent visit to the Musical Instrument
Museum, visitors played a large wooden drum.
Another man strummed a guitar. A woman and her
daughter listened to **music** from Africa and Asia.
The visitors to this museum in Phoenix, Arizona,
are here to experience and learn about different
sounds. At this museum, you're supposed to be loud!

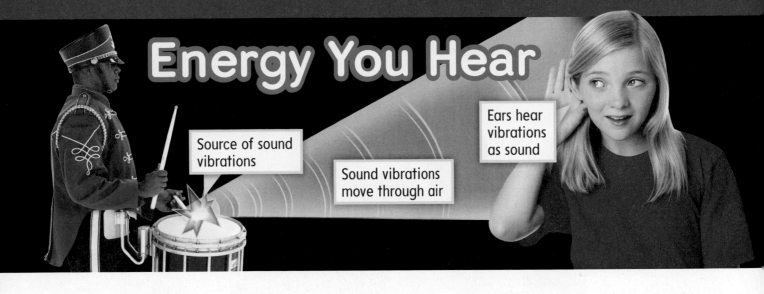

Energy You Hear

Source of sound vibrations

Sound vibrations move through air

Ears hear vibrations as sound

Humans can hear almost every **sound** in nature. But some animals hear sounds you can't hear. Dogs and bats, for example, can hear very high sounds that don't reach human ears. What sounds do you like to listen to?

Sound is the energy things make when they move back and forth. Those back and forth movements are called vibrations. Vibrations are like waves. When something vibrates, it makes the air vibrate, too. The waves move through the air quickly. We can hear the vibrations when the waves reach our ears. Our ears hear the waves as sounds.

Make Connections

How does sound help you express yourself? ESSENTIAL QUESTION

How do people express themselves through music? TEXT TO TEXT

Rain Forests

By Nancy Smiler Levinson

Illustrated by Diane Dawson Hearn

Essential Question

What makes different parts of the world different?

Read about the different plants and animals that live in rain forests.

Go Digital!

A rain forest is a wet forest. It is thick with many kinds of trees and plants. Many animals live in it. Rain falls most of the year.

Most rain forests grow in hot places near the equator. They are tropical rain forests. Some grow in cool places. They are **temperate** rain forests.

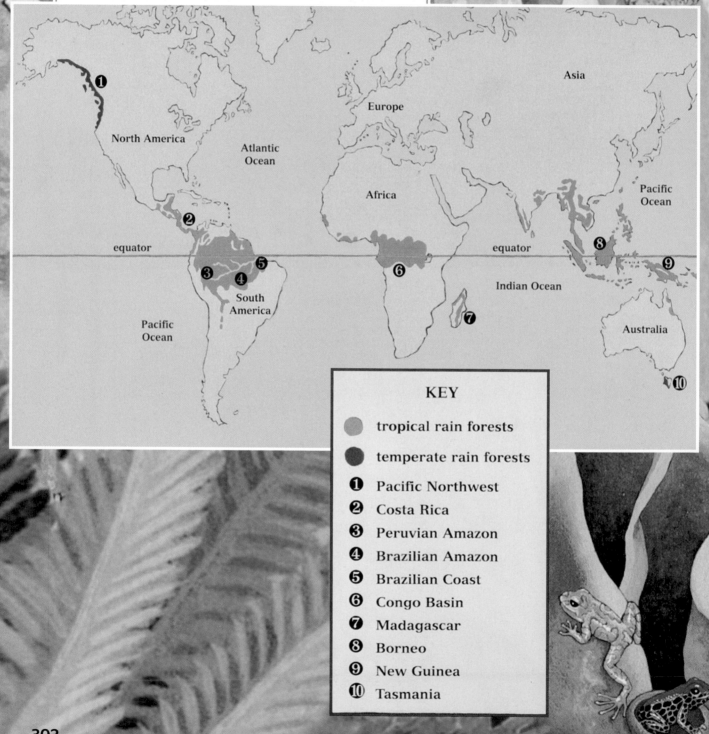

KEY

- tropical rain forests
- temperate rain forests

❶ Pacific Northwest
❷ Costa Rica
❸ Peruvian Amazon
❹ Brazilian Amazon
❺ Brazilian Coast
❻ Congo Basin
❼ Madagascar
❽ Borneo
❾ New Guinea
❿ Tasmania

Tropical Rain Forests

Tropical rain forests are hot and wet. How much rain falls every year? Between 80 and 200 inches! The temperatures stay almost the same every day. It is summer all the time.

Tropical rain forests are jungles. They are filled with trees, plants, and vines. Thousands of kinds of animals live in them.

One scientist found forty-three kinds of insects on one tree! The world's largest tropical rain forest is in the Amazon **region** of South America.

emergent

harpy eagles

ipe tree

blue-headed parrots

304

Rain forests have four **layers**.
Each layer has its own life-forms.
The top layer is called *emergent*. The
emergent trees poke above the rest
of the forest into the sunlight. Eagles
and parrots live there.

red howler
monkeys

kapok
treetop

canopy

The second layer is a closed *canopy.* It is a living roof that covers the forest below. It is formed by treetops that grow close together.

scarlet macaws

tayra

wasp

Monkeys eat berries and fruits.
Butterflies and hummingbirds drink
nectar from flowers. Big stinging
wasps crawl across leaves. This is
the most **lively** layer of all.

pygmy
marmoset

orchid

yolk
butterfly

swallowtail
hummingbird

squirrel
monkey

understory

cannonball
tree

coatimundi

bare-faced
curassow

collared
puffbird

passion
flower vine

jaguar

staghorn
fern

morpho
butterfly

palm
fern

The third layer is the *understory*.
It gets little sunlight. Sun cannot get
through the canopy. Few flowers
grow. Jaguars wait in trees to leap
down and catch prey on the ground.

forest floor

hoatzin
and baby

green
anaconda

moss

Victoria
amazonia
water lily

310

The fourth layer is the *forest floor*.
It is dark and **eerie**. It is filled with
plants, mosses, ferns, dead leaves,
and billions of ants.

capybara

ground
fern

caiman

apple snail

brocket
deer

saddleback
caterpillar

pink-toed
tarantula

heliconia

army ants

stink
beetle

Army ants march in swarms and eat
everything in their paths. Termites live
in colonies and eat wood. Deer and
wild pigs are hard to see, but insects
can be seen everywhere!

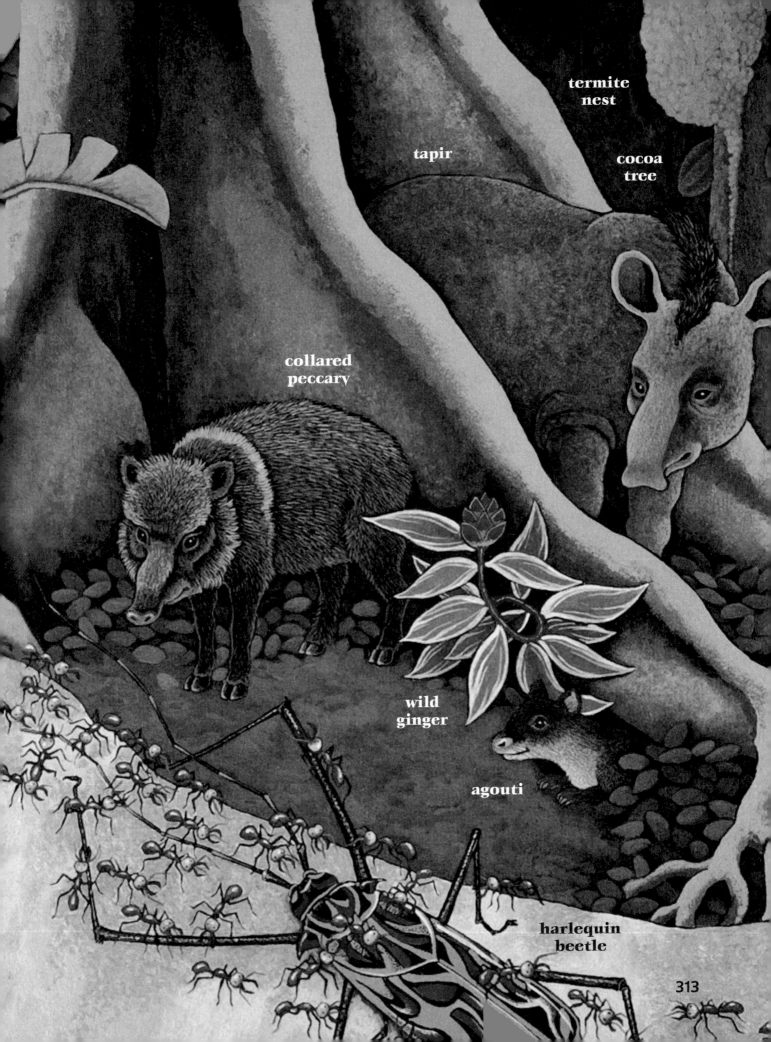

termite
nest

tapir

cocoa
tree

collared
peccary

wild
ginger

agouti

harlequin
beetle

313

three-toed
sloth

eyelash
viper

Many animals live in the trees most of their lives. Some tree frogs never touch the ground. They have sticky toe pads to help them climb slippery leaves. Sloths hang upside down all the time — even when they eat and sleep.

STOP AND CHECK

Reread Why do some tree frogs never touch the ground? Reread to check your understanding.

glass
frog

Most plants need roots in soil to get water and food. Air plants do not. They grow on tree trunks and get water and food from the air. They are called *epiphytes*. Orchids and bromeliads are epiphytes.

capuchin monkey

gladiator tree frog

315

northern
spotted owl

Sitka spruce

bald eagle

Temperate Rain Forests

Most temperate rain forests grow in the Pacific Northwest of North America. How much rain falls every year? About 100 inches! The **seasons** do change.

Fog and mist from the Pacific Ocean bring warm summers and cool winters. Temperate rain forests have layers, too. But they do not look like tropical rain forests. Sun rays shine down to the forest floor. Some trees are giant old-**growth** trees. A Sitka spruce may be a thousand years old!

mule deer

cougar

black bear cub

STOP AND CHECK

Ask and Answer Questions
How do temperate rain forests look different from tropical ones? Go back to the text to find the answer.

raven

Tongass National Forest in Alaska is the largest temperate rain forest in the United States. Rain forests grow along the western side of the Olympic Peninsula in Washington State, too. Most animals, such as squirrels, elks, and porcupines, live on the forest floor. The Olympic forest is alive with plants, too.

elk

bobcat

raccoon

skunk cabbage

devil's club

About the Author and Illustrator

Nancy Smiler Levinson

became interested in writing children's books when she began reading to her kids. Nancy likes to research and write nonfiction books because they let her share the things that interest her. She also writes fiction. People sometimes ask her whether she likes writing fiction or nonfiction best. She usually replies, "Both!"

Diane Dawson Hearn

has illustrated more than fifty books. Diane draws everything from funny cartoon characters to beautiful pictures of real plants and animals. She worked for two years on the illustrations for *Rain Forests*.

Author's Purpose

How does Nancy use diagrams and illustrations to help you understand the layers of the rain forest?

Respond to the Text

Summarize

Use important details from *Rain Forests* to summarize the selection. Information from your Compare and Contrast chart may help you.

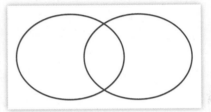

Write

How does the author organize the information about tropical rain forests? Use these sentence starters:

The author discusses the forest layers...
The author describes animals and plants...
The author uses diagrams and illustrations to show...

Make Connections

What makes rain forests different? **ESSENTIAL QUESTION**

Tell about a plant or animal you learned about that lives in the rain forest. **TEXT TO WORLD**

African Savannas

Plants and Animals

A savanna is a special **region** in Africa. In this part of Africa tall grasses grow. The savanna does not have groups of trees like in a forest. It has lots of single trees scattered across the grassland. Acacia (uh kay shuh) trees grow in the savanna. They have huge thorns. The leaves of this tree are a favorite food for giraffes. Baobab (bay oh bab) trees grow here, too. They are some of the oldest trees in the world. They can grow to be as wide as a house! Just one baobab can be a home for lizards, snakes, frogs, and birds for their entire life.

Many different kinds of animals live in the savanna. Zebras, lions, and meerkats all make the savanna their home.

Herds of zebra roam the savanna. Here they are next to an acacia tree.

(bkgd) James Warwick/Photographer's Choice/Getty Images (inset) imagebroker/Alamy

320

There are more types of hoofed animals in the African savanna than anywhere else in the world. Elephants, antelopes, giraffes, buffaloes, and rhinos are just some of the hoofed animals found in the savanna.

Seasons

Think about where you live. What is the weather like in each season? African savannas have a rainy season and a dry season. During the rainy season, it may rain for hours each day. The rain lasts for months. Then, there may be five months with no rain at all.

An African savanna is near the Equator, the imaginary line that is in the middle of Earth. That makes a savanna a warm **location** all year. A savanna is a special place, filled with interesting animals and plants.

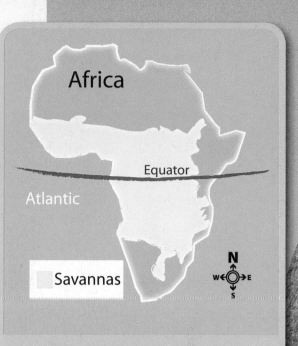

Savannas cover more than two-fifths of Africa.

Make Connections

What makes an African savanna different? ESSENTIAL QUESTION

How are a savanna's land features different from those of another region you have read about? TEXT TO TEXT

Adam Bennie/Vetta/Getty Images.

Genre • Expository Text

Essential Question
How does the Earth change?
Read about how volcanoes change the Earth.

Go Digital!

Volcanoes

by Sandra Markle

One ordinary April day, something special happened. Hot liquid rock **exploded** from a volcano on Iceland. Once in the air, the bits of liquid quickly cooled and turned into ash. Then the volcano kept on erupting. Soon the air was full of ash.

Nearby, a dairy farmer herded his cows into the family's big barn. His wife said, "It was scary. I could hear the volcano rumbling like distant thunder. Soon, even though It was day, it was dark. And there were flakes falling from the sky. These were not white snowflakes, though. The flakes were black. When they touched my skin, they felt like sand."

This volcano's eruption had a big impact on the **local** people and others around the world. So why did the volcano erupt?

Compared to the whole **Earth**, the Earth's crust is thin. The crust is broken into pieces like a cracked hardboiled egg. Each piece is called a plate. Deep inside, the Earth's core is so hot the rock around it heats up and moves.

As the rock heats up it rises. Near the crust, the rock cools off. Then it sinks. Scientists think these currents make the plates move. When the plates move, melted rock inside the earth rises. This melted rock is called magma.

Below the ground and water, the Earth's crust is broken into plates. Plates are on the move, but we can't feel it. The fastest plate moves just 6 inches each year.

See Magma for Yourself!

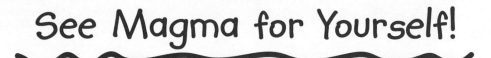

You can model what's happening to the magma under the Earth's plates.

- With an adult's help, boil water in a pot.

- Drop a handful of raisins into the water.

- Watch. You'll see the raisins sink and rise. The water heats up at the bottom of the pan and rises. It cools at the surface and sinks. The raisins ride the currents. The currents move the magma under the Earth's crust.

If the plates move far enough apart, magma reaches the Earth's surface. Magma may explode into the air. It may flow onto the Earth's surface. When magma flows out it is called lava.

Lava flows out at different places around the world. If a lot of lava flows out at one spot on the Earth's surface, it forms a mountain— a volcano. Many are along the edge of the Pacific Ocean. No wonder this is said to be a ring of fire!

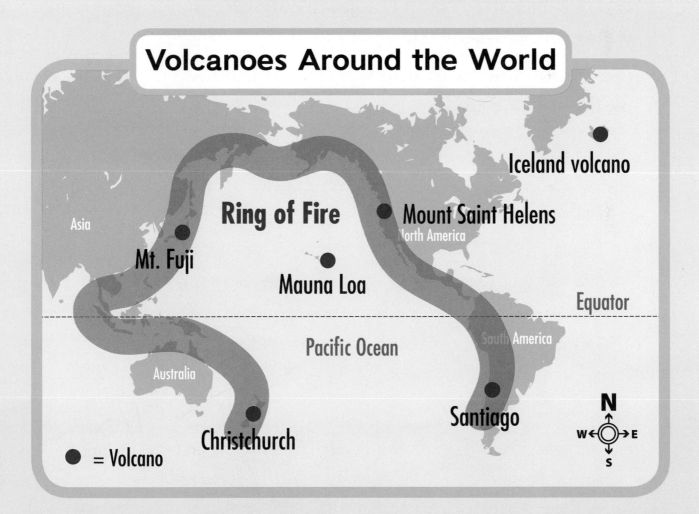

Volcanoes Around the World

Iceland volcano

Asia

Ring of Fire

Mount Saint Helens

North America

Mt. Fuji

Mauna Loa

Equator

Pacific Ocean

South America

Australia

Santiago

N
W ← → E
S

Christchurch

● = Volcano

Lava may have different **properties**, like being runny or stiff. If the lava is runny, it spreads out on the Earth's surface before it cools and becomes **solid**. This kind of lava forms a flat, shield-shaped volcano. Mauna Loa in Hawaii is a shield-shaped volcano. It started when lava poured out of an opening on the ocean floor. Then lava built up in layers. Once the mountaintop was above water, it formed an **island**. Mauna Loa continues to be very **active**. It has erupted 39 times since 1832.

Mauna Loa in Hawaii is the Earth's largest volcano.

This is the volcano that erupted in Iceland.

If the lava is stiff, it piles up on the Earth's surface and forms a cone-shaped volcano with **steep** sides. The volcano that erupted on Iceland is a cone-shaped volcano. It is not very active. Its last eruption was almost 200 years ago. While it was inactive, a lot of ice built up on the mountain. Then, in 2009, scientists discovered the volcano was becoming active again.

STOP AND CHECK

Reread What two shapes are volcanoes? Reread the text to find the answer.

David Forster/Alamy Stock Photo

327

Magma fills a chamber inside the volcano. Then it pushes up a pipe-like part to the opening at the surface, the crater.

Scientists know a volcano is getting ready to erupt when it swells. This happens because magma pushes up inside the volcano. The mountain does not swell enough for people to see it getting bigger. Special instruments measure the tiny movements of the rocks. Other instruments record earthquakes around the volcano. Lots of quakes are another clue magma is rising inside the volcano.

The Iceland volcano erupted lava under its ice covering. The ice melted and turned to steam. If you've ever watched steam lift the lid on a boiling pot, you know what happened next. Steam and gas escaping from the volcano blew magma high into the air. The magma exploded into millions of tiny droplets. These cooled and became ash. Winds carried the volcanic ash across Europe.

The volcanic ash could damage jet engine parts. So it was too dangerous to fly. Airplanes around the world were grounded. Some people were stranded.

After the eruption in Iceland, ash covered the ground.

Not just volcanic ash causes problems. Hot lava from volcanoes also creates damage. Flowing lava can destroy buildings and roads. The volcano named Mount Saint Helens in Washington state once blasted out hot gas and knocked down whole forests.

STOP AND CHECK

Reread How can volcanoes cause problems? Reread the text to find the answer.

Here a farmer is sweeping ash off of his roof.

Of course, the results of volcanic eruptions aren't all bad. For one thing, volcanoes build new mountains and islands. In Iceland, scientists discovered the bits of volcanic ash were coated with minerals plants need to grow. After the eruption, the dairy farmer had a big job cleaning ash off his house and barn roofs. In the fields, though, the grass quickly shot up healthy and green. Soon there was plenty of fresh food for his cows.

The ash makes a healthy place for plants to grow.

About the Author

Sandra Markle writes books, creates TV shows, and develops online programs on all kinds of science topics. She has had many exciting adventures doing research for them. Sandra watched active volcanoes in Hawaii, New Zealand, and Antarctica. "I never miss a chance to investigate volcanoes," says Sandra. "They are dramatic proof that the Earth is an ever-changing place!"

Author's Purpose

Sandra begins this selection by telling about the dairy farmer and his wife. How does their story help you understand what happens when a volcano erupts?

Respond to the Text

Summarize

Use important details to summarize what happens in the selection. Information from your Cause and Effect chart may help you.

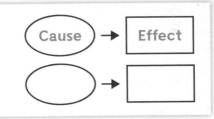

Write

How does the author help you understand the power of a volcano's eruption? Use these sentence starters:

The author compares...
She also includes...

Make Connections

How do volcanoes change the Earth?
ESSENTIAL QUESTION

What did you learn about volcanoes from the photos in this selection? **TEXT TO WORLD**

Compare Texts
Read about wildfire rescues.

To the Rescue

Wildfires are big fires that happen in open areas like forests. One **property** of a wildfire is that people have a hard time stopping them because they spread quickly. They can be caused by weather events like lightning or *droughts*, times when there isn't much rain. Hot, dry winds push the fires around.

Wildfires make many changes to the **Earth**. Some changes you see right away. Trees, crops, and other plants are burned. Other changes you see later on. Different plants might grow back.

People Rescues

Sometimes it is not safe for people to stay in their homes when a wildfire is nearby. Firefighters warn people about the fires.

If a fire gets too close, firefighters tell people that they need to leave their homes. Sometimes a fire can prevent people from driving away. Then firefighters might use a helicopter to fly people to safety.

Animal Rescues

Most animals know how to get away from fire by running, flying, or burrowing into the ground. Animals that are too young or injured might not escape. Rescuers help those animals get away. They might bring them to a wildlife *shelter*. People there treat animals that were hurt by the fire or smoke. Working together, people help others and animals stay safe from wildfires.

A rescuer named David Tree saved this koala named Sam.

Make Connections

? How does the Earth change after a wildfire? ESSENTIAL QUESTION

How are the changes to the Earth caused by volcanoes and wildfires alike and different? TEXT TO TEXT

Dear Primo
A Letter to My Cousin

By Duncan Tonatiuh

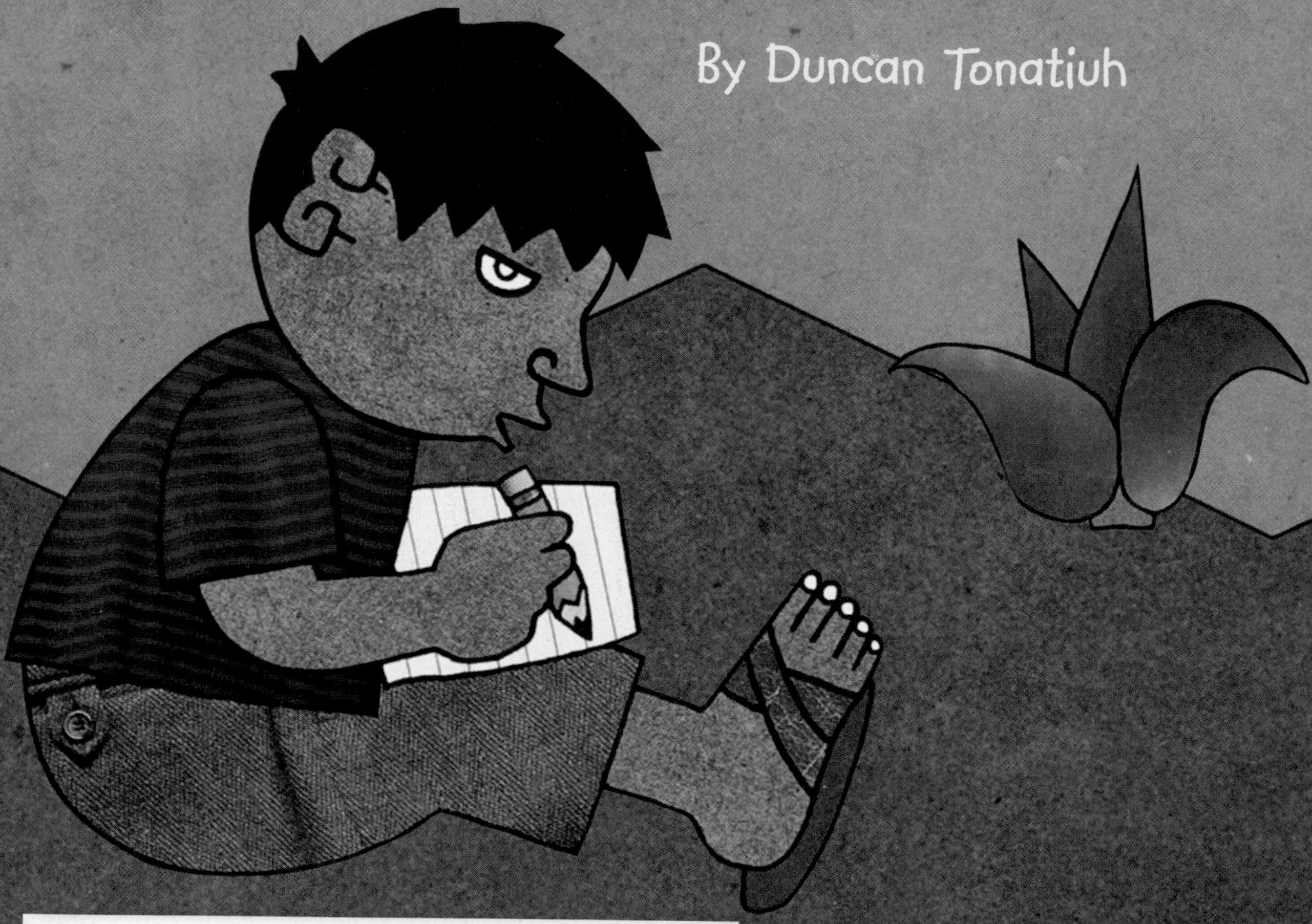

Essential Question
How are kids around the world different?

Read about how two cousins live and play in America and Mexico.

Go Digital!

Score! I just got a letter from my *primo*, my cousin, Carlitos. I live in America, but he lives in Mexico, where my family is from. Maybe someday we'll meet!

Dear Primo Charlie,

How are you? Do you **wonder** like me what life is like far away? I live on a farm **surrounded** by mountains and trees. My family grows many things, such as *maíz*.

We have a *burro, pollos,* and a *gallo.* Every morning the *gallo* crows and crows.

gallo

maíz

burro

pollos

Dear Primo Carlitos,

I live in a city. From my window I can see a bridge and cars zooming by. I can see skyscrapers, too.

Skyscrapers are buildings so tall they tickle the clouds. At night all the lights from the city look like stars from the sky.

Every morning I ride my *bicicleta* to school.

I ride it past the *perros* and past a *nopal.*

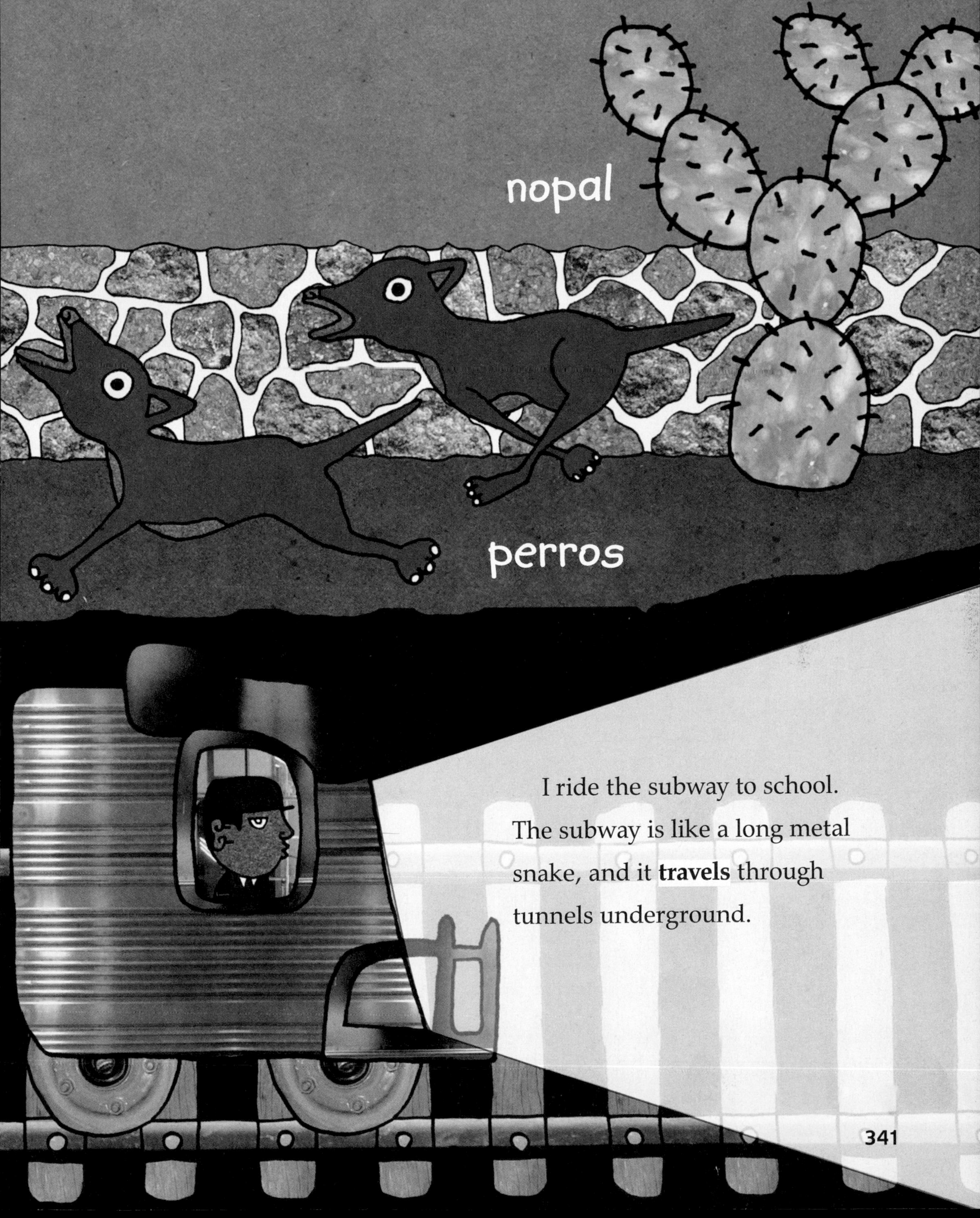

nopal

perros

I ride the subway to school.
The subway is like a long metal
snake, and it **travels** through
tunnels underground.

At recess time I play *fútbol*. My friend passes me the ball, I kick it with my foot, and if I score, I yell . . . *gol!*

I play basketball.
My friend dribbles
the ball and passes it
to me. I jump and shoot.

The ball goes *swoosh!*

Nothing but net.

When I come home from school, I help my mom cook. My **favorite** meal is *quesadillas*. I make them with cheese and *tortillas*.

quesadillas

tortillas

344

In America we have lots of different foods. My favorite is pizza. I like getting a slice on my way home from school.

After I finish my homework, my mom lets me go outside and play. In Mexico we have many games, like *trompos* and *canicas*.

trompo

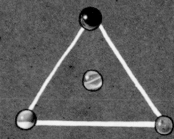
canicas

My favorite game is *papalotes.* My friends and I run and run, and with a little wind we fly the *papalote* high up.

papalote

When I finish my homework, I play games with my friends from the building. We play by the stoop . . .

. . . and in each other's apartments, too. I like going over to my friend's home to play video games.

río

In the afternoon it often gets hot. To cool off I jump in a small *río* that is nearby.

Visualize What do the cousins like to do when it is hot? Use the Visualize strategy to help you.

In the summer the city gets hot, too. I like getting splashed by the fire hydrant when the firefighters open it up and close off the block.

On the weekend I go with my parents to the *mercado,* an open-air market in the town nearby. We sell *maíz* and *tunas,* a prickly fruit that we grow. We also buy the food and other things we need.

maíz

tunas

On the weekend I go with my mom to the supermarket. She brings a list—milk, toothpaste, soap—and I check off the items as we put them in our cart.

2.00

In the town from time to time they have *fiestas* that last two or three days. At night there are *cohetes* that light up the sky and *mariachis* that play and play.

cohetes

mariachis

In my city sometimes we have **parades**. People in **costumes** and uniforms march down the street, and everyone gathers around to watch.

There are *charros* in Mexico that I wish you could see. They do tricks with their *caballos* and *reatas.*

charros

reata

caballo

On the streets here you can see break-dancers who do flips and spin on their heads.

In Mexico we have so many traditions,
such as the *Día de los Muertos,* the Day of
the Dead.

My favorite tradition is attending the December parties called *Posadas.* At the end of each *Posada* there is a *piñata* filled with fruit and sweets. When someone breaks it, we all get to jump in.

STOP AND CHECK

Reread What **customs** does the primo celebrate? Reread to check your understanding.

piñata

In America we have traditions, too, such
as Thanksgiving, when we eat turkey . . .

. . . and Halloween, when we dress up and go trick-or-treating. But I have to stop writing now. My mom just told me I have to brush my teeth and go to bed.

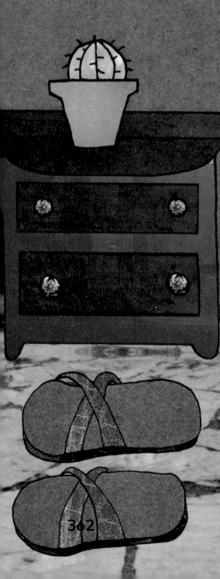

I have

My *primo* should come visit me!

an idea!

My *primo* should come visit me!

About the Author and Illustrator

Duncan Tonatiuh made his own comic books, drew cartoons of his friends, and also painted pictures as a child. Now Duncan writes and illustrates books.

When Duncan creates a book, he starts with an idea. For *Dear Primo,* he had the idea of two cousins writing to each other. He wanted readers to understand that people everywhere are more alike than different. Next Duncan writes and rewrites the story. Then he draws the pictures. Sometimes Duncan puts the book aside for months before he looks at it again. He may have a new idea about the story and want to change things. Finally he finishes the illustrations. Then the book is ready to be published!

Author's Purpose

Duncan uses Spanish words throughout the story. How does this help you understand what Carlitos is writing about in his letters?

Respond to the Text

Summarize

Use important details to summarize what happens in the story. Information from your Compare and Contrast chart will help you.

	Carlitos	Charlie
where they live		
games they play		

Write

How does the author show that Carlitos and Charlie are similar even though they live in different countries?

The author uses illustrations to show...
The author uses words to show...

Make Connections

What are some different customs of Carlitos and Charlie? ESSENTIAL QUESTION

Tell about a Mexican custom you read about in *Dear Primo*. TEXT TO WORLD

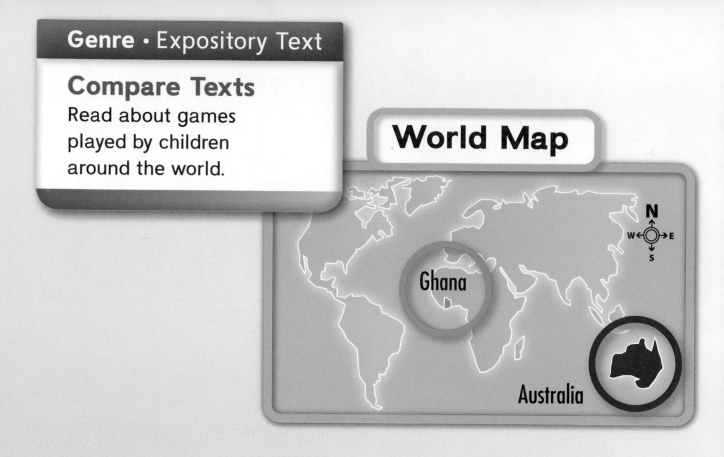

World Map

Ghana

Australia

Games Around the WORLD

What games do you and your friends like to play? Do you like outdoor games where you move around? Maybe you like to play board or computer games together indoors.

Kids around the world play different games together. Games are part of a country's **customs**. Here are some of the games kids play in countries around the world.

Stuck in the Mud

Tag is a **common** kind of game. Children all around the world play tag games. Kids in Australia play a tag game called "stuck in the mud." One person is "it." This person tags other players. A tagged player must freeze in place, as if stuck in sticky mud. Other players can free a tagged player. To free a player, you crawl between that person's feet. The game ends when everyone is stuck in the mud.

These children in Australia are playing "stuck in the mud."

Oware

Children in Ghana play a board game called *oware* (oh-wah-ruh). Oware is one of the oldest games in the world that people still play. Two players use a wooden game board with 12 small cups in it. Players have 48 game pieces. Usually, these are nuts, beans, or pebbles. Players must plan how to move the pieces from cup to cup. The game helps you become good at math.

These boys from Ghana are playing *oware*.

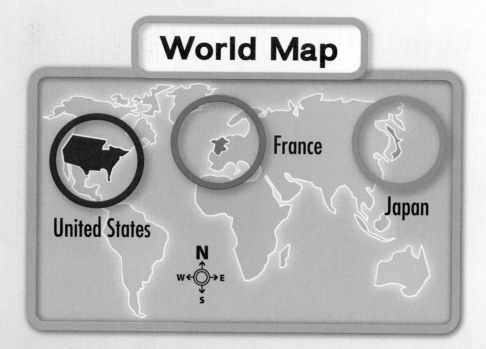

World Map

United States

France

Japan

N
W ←◇→ E
S

Jump Rope

Boys and girls around the world have played *jump rope* for hundreds of years. All you need is a piece of rope! Settlers from the Netherlands brought this game to America long ago.

Today some games are played with more than one rope. Jumpers can do tricks like twists and turns. There are even contests to see who can jump the most times or do the best tricks.

In this game of jump rope, the girl in the middle has to jump over two ropes.

Snail

Children in France play the game *snail*. It is like American hopscotch. Children draw a large snail on the ground with chalk. They mark off boxes inside its shell. Then kids hop to the center. Players can't put both feet down or they lose a turn.

The children playing *snail* must hop on one foot through the chalk snail.

Ayatori

In Japan, kids play a game with string called *ayatori* (ay-uh-toh-ree). To play, kids make a loop with the string. Then they wrap the string around their fingers to make shapes. For example, they make the string look like a broom or a ladder. The game is played alone or with a friend.

These children are playing *ayatori*.

Kids around the world play different games. No matter where they live, they know how to have fun!

Make Connections

How are the games that kids around the world play different? **ESSENTIAL QUESTION**

How are these games similar to the games kids play in *Dear Primo*? **TEXT TO TEXT**

Essential Question

How can we understand nature?

Read about how a beetle got its bright colors.

Go Digital!

HOW THE BEETLE GOT HER COLORS

BASED ON A TRADITIONAL TALE FROM BRAZIL

By Joseph Bruchac

Illustrated by Mercedes McDonald

Folktales teach us useful lessons and share **wisdom** with us. They explain things about the natural world. This folktale tells how beetles got such bright colors. The story comes from the rain forests of Brazil. That is the setting of this play. Many different plants and animals make their home in the rain forest. Some of those animals are the characters in this play.

CHARACTERS:

Narrator: A human storyteller

Beetle:
A gray-colored insect

Arrow Frog:
A very brightly colored frog

Agouti (uh-goo-tee):
A rodent animal with
glossy brown fur

Jaguar (jag-wahr):
A black and gold
spotted animal

Parrot:
A bird with feathers
of red and blue and gold

Anaconda:
A big snake with
patterns on his back

Narrator: Long ago, Beetle did not look the way she does today. Agouti made fun of her.

Agouti: Beetle, you are not beautiful like me. I have lovely brown fur. It shines in the light. You are just plain gray.

Beetle: I don't mind being gray.

Agouti: Hah! You are the plainest animal in the forest. You do not have beautiful gold and black spots like Jaguar.

Jaguar: That's true. I do have beautiful black and gold spots.

Agouti: You don't have shiny designs on your skin like Arrow Frog.

Arrow Frog: That is true. I do have shiny designs on my skin.

Agouti: You do not have interesting shapes on your body like Anaconda.

Anaconda: Yesssss, the shapes on my body are very interesting. Would you like to come clossser and look at them, Parrot?

Parrot: No, thank you. I will stay up here in the tree.

Agouti: You do not have feathers of red and blue and gold and green like Parrot.

Parrot: That's true. But it's not nice to **boast** about being better than someone else. Stop teasing poor Beetle.

Beetle: I do not like being teased. It makes me sad.

Agouti: We are all good-looking and you are plain. I can see why you hide in the bushes all day. You may be gray, but I bet you feel blue!

STOP AND CHECK

Visualize How does Beetle look different from the other animals? Use the Visualize strategy to help you.

Narrator: Agouti kept teasing poor little Beetle. Agouti boasted about how good-looking he was. Parrot did not like Agouti's teasing. She got tired of hearing Agouti boast. Finally, from the top of the tree Parrot gave a loud **holler**.

Parrot: Hey, hey! Hold your tongue, Agouti. All you animals, listen. I propose a race between Beetle and Agouti.

Agouti: Will there be a prize for the winner?

Parrot: I will give a beautiful new coat of any color to the winner.

Beetle: Even though I am happy being gray, a pretty new coat would be nice.

Agouti: Ha! I'll win this race. I have four fast, strong legs. Beetle, all you do is creep along on your six little skinny ones. You will be far behind when I **dash** across the finish line!

Beetle: I may surprise you.

Agouti: Ha! I do not think so.

Parrot: Beetle and Agouti, are you ready?

Agouti: I am ready. You will all see how fast I am.

Beetle: I am ready, too. I will try my best.

Parrot: Then let the race begin. Go!

Arrow Frog: Agouti is really fast. Look at him go!

Jaguar: Beetle is hardly moving. Agouti is far ahead of her.

Anaconda: Yesss, but what is Beetle doing now? What are thossse thingsss on Beetle's back?

Parrot: Just watch and see.

Arrow Frog: Wow! Look at that!

Jaguar: I have never seen anything like that before.

Anaconda: Yesss! That is amazing.

Agouti: I'm so fast that I left that silly little beetle far behind. What color shall I have Parrot paint me? Red? Green? Blue? How about red and blue with green spots? I will choose **plenty** of colors. I will look so beautiful. Ah, there is the finish line!

Arrow Frog: Agouti, where were you?

Jaguar: Beetle got here long ago.

Anaconda: Beetle wasssss very fasssst. You should have sssseen her.

Parrot: Beetle won the race. She has achieved **victory**!

Agouti: You won! How did you get here so fast?

Beetle: I flew. See my wings?

Agouti: I did not know you could fly.

Parrot: You should never judge anyone by the way they look. Even a plain little creature may have some hidden power.

STOP AND CHECK

Visualize How did Beetle's wings help her win the race? Use the Visualize strategy to help you.

Narrator: Agouti was so **ashamed** that he crawled off and hid while Beetle got her colors. She chose to be as green as the forest trees and as gold as the bright sun in the sky. And that is how she looks to this day.

Beetle: I am beautiful.

Narrator: A story such as this is fun to hear, but it also teaches us a useful lesson. The tale of Agouti and Beetle shows us the wisdom of not making fun of others.

ABOUT THE AUTHOR AND ILLUSTRATOR

JOSEPH BRUCHAC started writing in the second grade. He wrote poems for his teacher. He also loved reading stories about animals, like the ones in *How the Beetle Got Her Colors*. Joseph has written over 70 books for children and adults. Many of the stories he tells are from Native American cultures.

MERCEDES MCDONALD has always loved to paint. By the age of three, she knew she was an artist! Mercedes says, "My art is inspired by my cats, my dog, and the beautiful animals I see in nature every day."

AUTHOR'S PURPOSE

This play has some lines in italics. They are called stage directions. Stage directions tell about the actions of the characters. Why do you think Joseph included stage directions in this play?

Respond to the Text

Summarize

Use important details to summarize what happens in the folktale. Your Theme chart will help you.

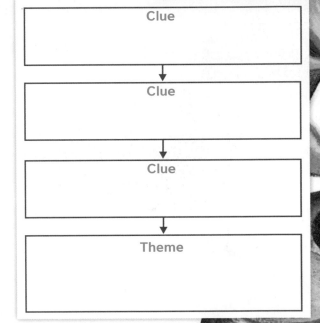

Clue

↓

Clue

↓

Clue

↓

Theme

Write

How has Agouti's character changed by the end of the story? Use these sentence starters:

> Agouti is different because . . .
> At the end Agouti realizes . . .

Make Connections

How did this selection help you understand nature?
ESSENTIAL QUESTION

What did you learn about beetles from this selection?
TEXT TO WORLD

Genre • Folktale

Compare Texts
Read about how a plain gray bird came to be so colorful.

How the Finch Got Its Colors

A Folktale from Belgium

Long ago, all birds looked alike. They all had wings, a beak, and the same gray feathers. Their **similarities** confused King Bird. He often called them the wrong names.

King Bird was a smart leader with great **wisdom**. He thought long and hard about the problem. Finally the answer came to him after a big storm left behind a rainbow.

King Bird called all the birds together. "Birds, look at this beautiful rainbow," he said. "I want you to be beautiful, too, so choose a color for your feathers."

The birds chirped and flapped. They also snatched at the colors.

Illustration Greg Newbold

"Orange and black are mine!" Robin sang.

"Blue, blue, I want blue!" Jay squawked.

Greedy hummingbird zoomed in. "I'm taking purple, green, and black," she hummed.

The birds proudly showed their new colors. Then King Bird noticed Finch hiding behind a tree, still dull and gray.

"Finch, where is your color?" he asked.

"I tried to get some, but I got pushed aside," Finch said sadly.

King Bird was angry, so he ordered each bird to pluck a single colorful feather and give it to Finch. Soon Finch was the most colorful bird of all. That is how the finch got its beautiful colors.

Make Connections

How does this folktale help us understand birds? **ESSENTIAL QUESTION**

What have you learned about nature from the stories you have read this week? **TEXT TO TEXT**

Essential Question

What excites us about nature?

Read how poems express what we love about the rain.

Go Digital!

382

April Rain Song

by Langston Hughes

Let the rain kiss you.

Let the rain beat upon your head with silver liquid **drops**.

Let the rain sing you a lullaby.

The rain makes still pools on the sidewalk.

The rain makes running pools in the gutter.

The rain plays a little sleep-song on our roof at night—

And I love the rain.

"April Rain Song" from THE COLLECTED POEMS OF LANGSTON HUGHES by Langston Hughes, edited by Arnold Rampersad with David Roessel, Associate Editor, copyright © 1994 by the Estate of Langston Hughes. Used by permission of Alfred A. Knopf, a division of Random House, Inc.

Rain Poem

by Elizabeth Coatsworth

The rain was like a little mouse,
quiet, small and gray.
It pattered all around the house
and then it went away.

It did not come, I understand,
indoors at all, until
it found an open window and
left tracks across the sill.

Respond to the Text

Summarize

Use important details from "April Rain Song" to describe the poem's theme. Information from your Theme chart may help you.

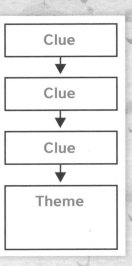

Clue
↓
Clue
↓
Clue
↓
Theme

Write

How do the literary elements help you understand the meaning of the poems? Use these sentence starters:

Comparing rain to a mouse shows...
Repeating the words "let the rain" tells...

Make Connections

What about rain excites you? ESSENTIAL QUESTION

Each poem describes the way the rain makes the speaker feel. How does the rain make you feel? TEXT TO WORLD

Helicopters

by Sylvia Cassedy

One day each spring,

and I never know

which day it will be,

the tree outside my

window

fills with a wind

all its own,

swells like a giant

silk parasol,

lets fall

a wondrous storm

of helicopters,

pale, pale green.

"Helicopters" by Sylvia Cassedy, from *Zoomrimes: Poems About Things That Go* (HarperCollins Publishers), ©1993 by the Estate of Sylvia Cassedy. Reprinted by permission of Ellen Cassedy.

Windy Tree

by Aileen Fisher

Think of the muscles

a tall tree grows

in its leg, in its foot,

in its wide-spread toes—

not to tip over

and fall on its nose

when a wild wind hustles

and tussles and blows.

Make Connections

The poems both describe what happens **outdoors** on a windy day. What **excites** you about the wind? ESSENTIAL QUESTION

"Helicopters" uses a simile to compare the tree to a parasol. What other similes have you read this week? TEXT TO TEXT

From IN THE WOODS, IN THE MEADOW, IN THE SKY by Aileen Fisher. Copyright © 1965, 1993 by Aileen Fisher. Used by permission of Marian Reiner on behalf of the Boulder Public Library Foundation, Inc.

GRACE
FOR
PRESIDENT

By KELLY DiPUCCHIO

Illustrated by LeUYEN PHAM

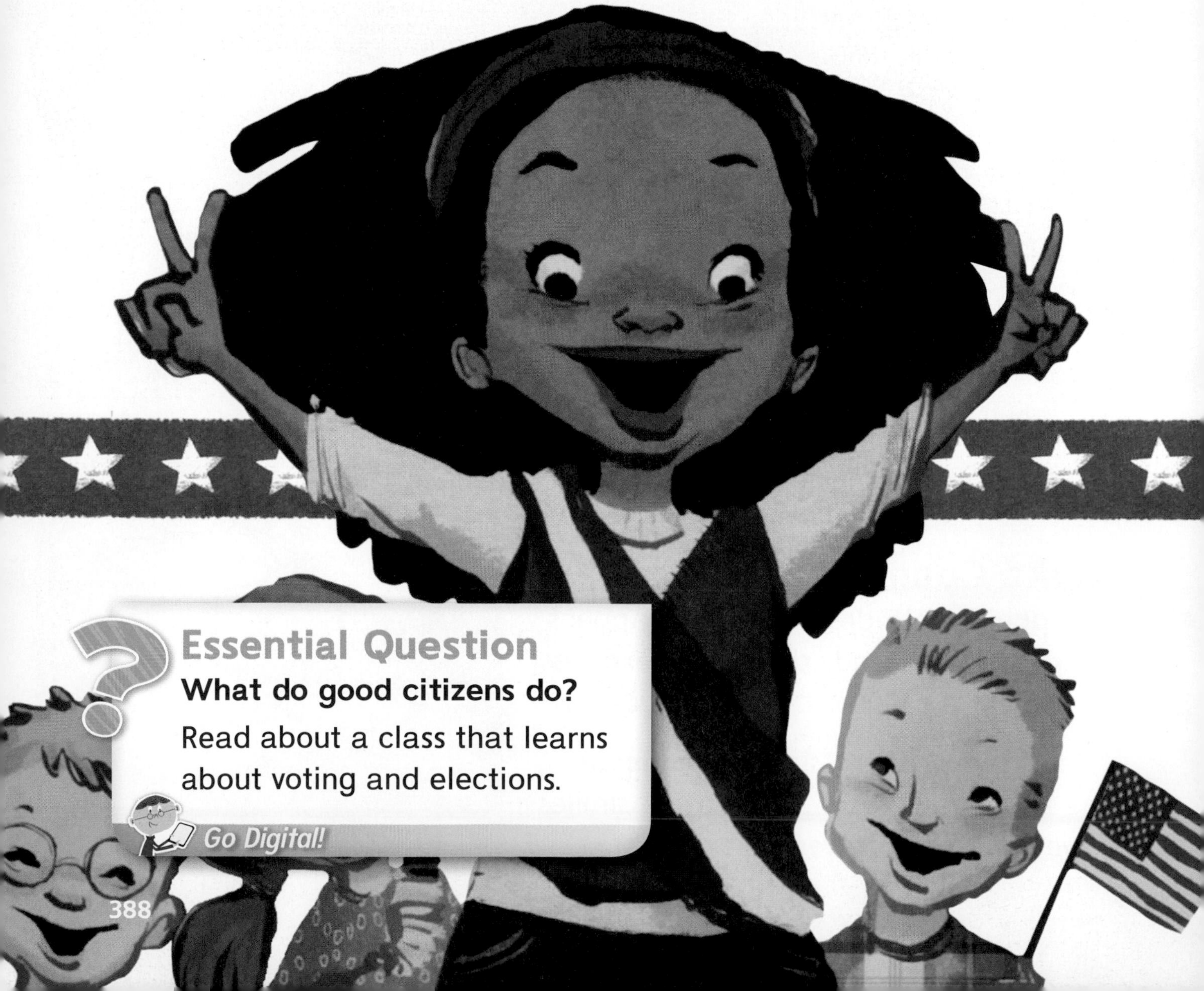

Go Digital!

Essential Question

What do good citizens do?

Read about a class that learns about voting and elections.

One Monday morning in September, Mrs. Barrington rolled out a big poster with all of the presidents' pictures on it. Grace Campbell could not believe her eyes.

"Where are the **GIRLS**?"

"That is a very good question!" said Mrs. Barrington. "The truth is, our country has never had a woman president."

"**NO** girl president? **EVER**?" Grace asked.

"No, I'm afraid not," said Mrs. Barrington.

Grace sat at her desk and stewed. No girls? Who'd ever heard of such a crazy thing?

Finally, she raised her hand.

"Yes, Grace?"

"I've been thinking it over, and I'd like to be **PRESIDENT**!"

Several students in the class laughed.

"Well, I think that's a star-spangled idea, Grace!" said Mrs. Barrington. "In fact, we can have our own election right here at Woodrow Wilson Elementary!"

The snickering in the room stopped. Grace smiled. "Would anyone else like to run for president?" Mrs. Barrington asked the class.

Nobody raised their hand.

Becoming president was going to be easy! Grace thought.

The next day, Mrs. Barrington made an announcement.

"In the name of **DEMOCRACY**, I have invited Mr. Waller's class to join our election. Their class has nominated **THOMAS COBB** to be their presidential candidate!"

Grace's heart sank.

Thomas was the school spelling bee champion. His experiments always took a blue ribbon at the science fair. And he was captain of the soccer team.

Becoming president wasn't going to be so easy, after all, Grace thought.

The teachers put the names of all fifty states
and the District of Columbia into a hat. Everyone
except for Grace and Thomas got to choose a state.

"I'm Texas!" said Anthony. "I'm New Hampshire!" said Rose. "I'm Michigan," said Robbie. "What does the number 17 mean?"

"Each state is assigned a number of electoral **votes**. That number is **determined** by how many people live in that state," said Mrs. Barrington. "Each of you will be a representative for your state."

"Altogether, our country has 538 electoral votes," Mr. Waller explained. "On election day, the candidate who receives 270 electoral votes or more wins the election!"

"Why 270?" asked Rose.

"That's more than half of all the electoral votes," Mr. Waller said.

Becoming president REALLY wasn't going to be so easy, Grace thought.

Grace came up with a campaign slogan:

Thomas came up with his own campaign slogan:

AKE HISTORY! VOTE **GRACE CAMPBELL** FOR PRESIDENT!

VOTE FOR **THOMAS COBB** THE BEST **MAN** FOR THE JOB!

Grace listened to what **issues** were important to the students, and she made a list of campaign **promises**:

Thomas made up his own list of promises:

Grace made campaign posters and buttons.

Thomas made posters and buttons, too.

Each week, the teachers set aside time for the candidates to meet with their constituents.

Polls were taken. Voters were making their choices.

Grace continued to campaign. At recess, she gave
SPEECHES. During lunch, she handed out free
CUPCAKES. After school, she held **RALLIES**.

STOP AND CHECK

Summarize How did Grace campaign to be president? Summarize what she did.

Arizona 10   Kentucky 8   N. Dakota 3
Arkansas 6   Louisiana 9   Ohio 20
California 55   Maine 4   Oklahoma 7
Colorado 9   Maryland 10   Oregon 7
Connecticut 7   Massachusetts 12   Pennsylvania 21
Delaware 3   Michigan 17   Rhode Island 4
D.C. 3   Minnesota 10   S. Carolina 8
Florida 27   Mississippi 6   S. Dakota 3
Georgia 15   Missouri 11   Tennessee 11
Hawaii 4   Montana 3   Texas 34
Idaho 4   Nebraska 5   Utah 5
Illinois 21   Nevada 5   Vermont 3
Indiana 11   New Hampshire 4   Virginia 13
Iowa 7   New Jersey 15   Washington 11
Kansas 6   New Mexico 5   W. Virginia 5
   New York 31   Wisconsin 10
   N. Carolina 15   Wyoming 3

271

MEANWHILE, Thomas wasn't worried.
He had cleverly calculated that the **BOYS**
held slightly more electoral votes than the **GIRLS**.
At recess, Thomas studied his spelling words.
During lunch, he worked on his latest science
experiment. After school, he played soccer.

Even before the election, Grace made good on her promises. She joined the safety squad. She organized a school beautification committee, and she **volunteered** her time in the school cafeteria.

In early November, Woodrow Wilson
Elementary hosted a special Election Day
assembly. Grace and Thomas took their places
onstage as the school band began to play.

Henry was the first representative to approach the microphone.

The Yellowhammer state of Alabama casts its 9 electoral votes for Thomas Cobb!

Fletcher said,

The Last Frontier State of Alaska casts its 3 electoral votes for the best man for the job, Thomas Cobb!

Hannah called out:

The Grand Canyon State of Arizona casts its 10 electoral votes for Grace Campbell!

And so it went. State after state after state cast their electoral votes. The scoreboard in the gymnasium kept track of the totals.

The voting demonstration was quickly coming to an end. Clara approached the podium.

The Badger State of Wisconsin casts its 10 votes for my best friend, Grace Campbell!

Grace looked at the scoreboard. Thomas had 268 electoral votes. She had 267. There was only one state still unaccounted for.

Wyoming.

Thomas grinned. Grace felt sick.

Sam walked up to the microphone.

He looked at Thomas.

He looked at Grace.

He looked down at Grace's handmade flag.

Sam didn't say a word.

"What are you waiting for?" Thomas whispered.

The band stopped playing.

All eyes were on Wyoming.

Finally, Sam cleared his throat.

The Equality State of Wyoming casts its three electoral votes for . . .

405

The gymnasium erupted in loud cheers (and a few boos).

Mrs. Barrington approached the podium.

"With 270 electoral votes, the winner is Grace Campbell!"

Thomas looked stunned. Grace hugged Sam.

"Why did you do it?" she asked.

Sam handed Grace his flag. "Because," he said. "I thought you were the best person for the job."

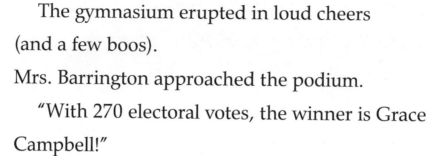

STOP AND CHECK

Visualize What happens in the gym after Grace's name is called? Use the Visualize strategy to help you.

The following week, the students in Mrs. Barrington's class were preparing for their Career Day presentations.

Grace volunteered to go first. She stood at the front of the room and glanced at the poster still hanging on the wall.

"My name is Grace Campbell, and when I grow up, I'm going to be president of the United States."

This time, everyone believed that she would.

About the Author and Illustrator

Kelly DiPucchio spent most of her childhood daydreaming. Unlike Grace, she never imagined that she would become president. Instead, she wanted to become a famous artist or singer. Today she is a famous author of award-winning picture books. Kelly lives with her family in Michigan, which has 17 electoral votes.

LeUyen Pham was born in Vietnam and grew up in the United States. She loves to travel the world. LeUyen visited five of the seven continents, rode an elephant, and got lost in Africa.

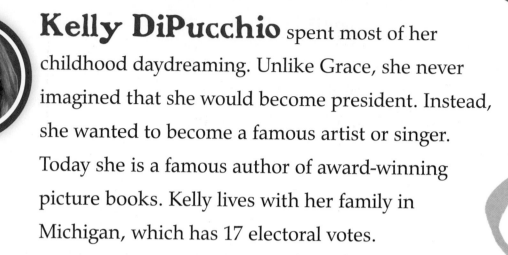

Author's Purpose

Kelly uses descriptive words to show what a character thinks or feels. What do you think Mrs. Barrington means when she says that Grace has a "star-spangled idea"?

Respond to the Text

Summarize

Use important details to summarize what happens in the story. Key information from your Point of View chart may help you.

Character	Setting	Point of View

Write

How does the author keep the reader interested as she tells her story about Grace's run for class president? Use these sentence starters:

The author uses text and illustrations to...
She helps me predict by...
She builds suspense by...

Make Connections

Why is voting the responsibility of a good citizen? ESSENTIAL QUESTION

What are some things you learned about what happens in an election? TEXT TO WORLD

Helping to Make Smiles

Matthew Stephenson lives in Texas. He has a disability. It makes his muscles weak. People with Matthew's disability can have trouble walking, sitting, and writing. Some use a wheelchair.

Camp Smiles

During the summer, Matthew goes to Camp Smiles. It is an Easter Seals camp for children with disabilities. Children with special needs often can't go to other camps. Other camps cannot help them meet their needs. At Camp Smiles, there is special gear. Each camper has a buddy to help him or her. Children at Camp Smiles are able to ride horses, play basketball, and swim. Camp may be the only place where they can do those activities.

Matthew Stephenson at Camp Smiles.

Camp Smiles camper, Matthew Stephenson and counselor, Tony Agosto

410

A Camp Smiles camper with her buddy.

Matthew's Camp Challenge

Matthew had a great time at Camp Smiles. He wanted other children like him to get to go to camp. Not all kids can afford to go to camp. Matthew wanted to change that. He decided to challenge people to give money. The money will pay for 30 children to go to Camp Smiles. Matthew showed **responsibility**. He is involved in his community. He is helping to make children with disabilities smile.

A good citizen is someone who is...

- Respectful of the rights of others
- Responsible
- Involved in his or her community
- Thoughtful of others' feelings

How are you a good citizen?

Make Connections

What makes Matthew a good citizen? **ESSENTIAL QUESTION**

What are some different ways that people can be good citizens? **TEXT TO TEXT**

Camp Smiles camper, Megan Fry, and counselor, Margaret Johnson

Once Upon a Baby Brother

By Sarah Sullivan

Pictures by Tricia Tusa

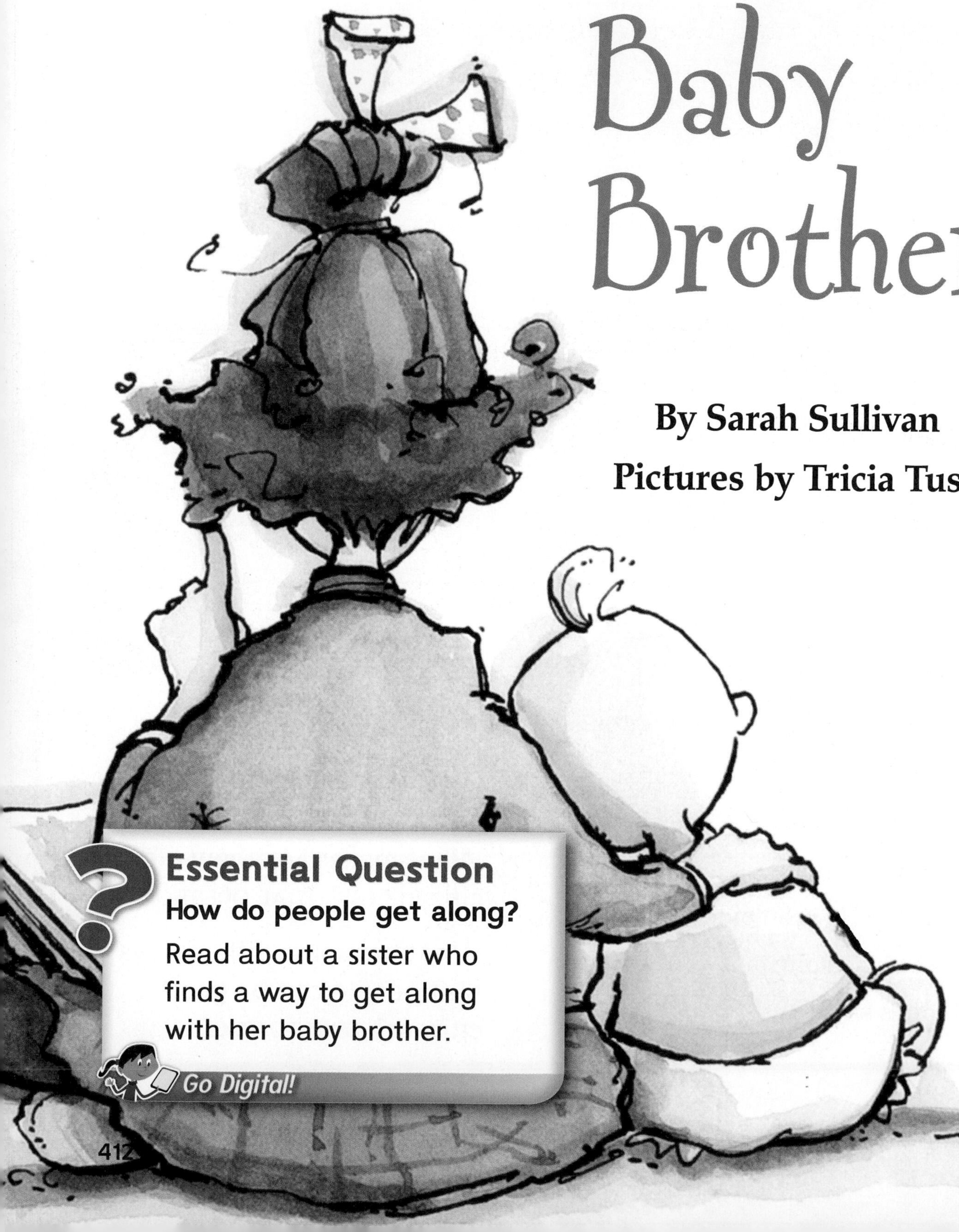

? Essential Question

How do people get along?

Read about a sister who finds a way to get along with her baby brother.

Go Digital!

412

From the day she could talk, Lizzie loved
to tell stories. Tall ones. True ones. Funny ones.
Sad ones. Lizzie loved them all.

She **entertained** the people in her mother's
office. *And the little girl grew up to be President and
brought her parents to live with her in the White House.*

She made up fairy tales to share with her father during their hikes up Mount Tilapia. *After slaying dragons in the forest, the princess gave a surprise birthday party for the king.*

She spun yarns for Big George. *The beautiful girl and her handsome dog took a rocket to the moon and discovered a new planet in the solar system.*

Everything was fine UNTIL
her little brother, Marvin, came along.

When Lizzie tried to tell a story before breakfast, her mother said, "Not now, dear. Marvin has a dirty diaper."

When she tried to tell her father a story after dinner, he said, "Maybe later, Lizzie. It's time for Marvin's bath."

Luckily for Lizzie, Big George still loved her stories. He would listen for hours. Stories about dogs were his favorite. *The faithful Labrador rescued his master from the storm-tossed seas.*

"Arf! Arf!"

When Lizzie started second grade, she discovered that her teacher, Miss Pennyroyal, loved stories, too. All the kids in Miss Pennyroyal's class got to write stories and take turns reading them out loud.

The brave young girl rescued her teacher from the alligator pit.

Lizzie loved Miss Pennyroyal's second grade.

At home, Marvin loved his big sister, Lizzie.

He helped her make her bed.

He helped her brush her teeth.
He even shared his oatmeal.

Lizzie couldn't wait to get to school every morning.

At school, Miss Pennyroyal taught her students how to create interesting characters. "Think about what makes your character different from everybody else," she said, "and **describe** that in your stories."

Easy peasy, thought Lizzie.

She got out her Princess Merriweather pencil. While the other kids brainstormed, Lizzie started writing.

She wrote all through recess.

She was still writing while the other kids ate lunch.

"Can I go first, please?" Lizzie asked when it was time to share stories out loud.

"There's only one creature with footprints like this, Captain."

"You don't mean . . ."

"I'm afraid so, sir. The Yeti is on the rampage again."

"Nice to see you using those new vocabulary words," said Miss Pennyroyal.

"Thank you," said Lizzie.

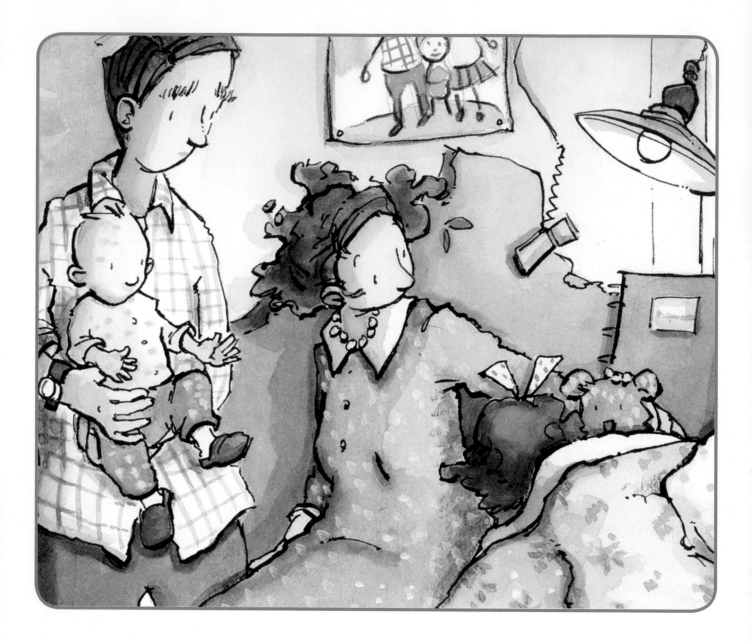

The next day, while Lizzie was at school, Marvin found a tube of golden glitter glue in Lizzie's desk drawer. He made golden glitter swirls all over her favorite stuffed bear, Sebastian. Lizzie was not **amused**.

"Big sisters need to be **patient**," said Lizzie's mother.

"Babies can't help making messes," said Lizzie's father.

Lizzie curled up in her bedroom with her **Imagination** Notebook and wrote a new story.

Once there was a beautiful princess who lived in a castle by the Sea. She made her parents very happy. THEN the ugly prince was born.

He cried ALL the time. And made lots of messes. So the beautiful princess banished the ugly prince to a desert island.

"This castle is way too getting crowded," she told her trusty steed.

Lizzie was happy to go to school the next day.

The kids in Miss Pennyroyal's class were still writing stories about interesting characters.

Lizzie had tons of ideas. It was hard to find time to write them all down.

Run for your lives!
It's the Marvinosaurus.

Marvin's the nastiest pirate that ever sailed the sea.

Watch your fingers!
There's a Marvinfish circling below.

"I don't believe I've ever heard of a Marvinfish,"
said Miss Pennyroyal. "It must be very rare."

"Oh, it is," said Lizzie. "You hardly ever see one."

On Friday, Lizzie's mother announced she
was taking Marvin to visit Gramma. "I hope you
won't miss your little brother too much," she said.
NO MARVIN!!
Lizzie was thrilled.

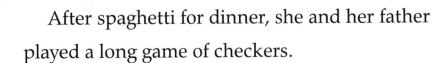

After spaghetti for dinner, she and her father played a long game of checkers.

The next afternoon, Lizzie sharpened a whole box of pencils.

She dusted the furniture in her Princess Merriweather Magic Castle.

She rearranged the stuffed animals on her bed twelve times.

But something was missing.

At school, Miss Pennyroyal announced a new project.

"Now that we know about creating characters, we're going to write our own comic books," she said. "Everyone needs to think of a character who will have lots of adventures."

Lizzie took out her Princess Merriweather pencil.

She doodled.

She stared out the window.

For the first time, she couldn't think of a single idea.

That night, while Lizzie's father worked on a sales report for his meeting, Lizzie tried to work on her comic book.

She drew stars on the cover of her Imagination Notebook.

She stared at a liver-shaped spot on the ceiling.

She even cleaned out her sock drawer.

"Once, in a far-off galaxy," she wrote. And then . . .

nothing!

The next day at school, the kids in Miss Pennyroyal's class turned in their comic book projects—everyone except Lizzie.

"Remember, the deadline is the day after tomorrow," said Miss Pennyroyal.

"I know," Lizzie moaned.

"Maybe you need fresh inspiration," said Miss Pennyroyal.

"Maybe," said Lizzie.

She chewed on the end of her Princess Merriweather pencil.

"It was a dark and stormy night," she wrote, and then . . .

nothing!

427

At home, Lizzie looked for inspiration.

She listened to music and drew pictures on blank sheets of paper.

She reread her favorite fairy tales.

She studied the comics in the Sunday paper.

Nothing helped.

"I'll never think of a character for my comic book," Lizzie moaned.

STOP AND CHECK

Summarize What did Lizzie do for inspiration? Summarize what she did.

She went downstairs for a glass of juice.

"Mug worts," said the chrysanthemum.

"Marvin?" said Lizzie. "When did you get home?"

"Ziff wizzle," said Marvin. Then he knocked over Lizzie's juice.

"Oh, Marvin!" said Lizzie.

"Loops," said Marvin.

Lizzie thought about Miss Pennyroyal's instructions: interesting characters . . . lots of adventures . . . Hmmm.

Lizzie carried her Princess Merriweather pencil upstairs.

She wrote until bedtime and while she was brushing her teeth.

She was still writing during recess the next day.

"Is your comic book ready to turn in?" asked Miss Pennyroyal.

"Not quite," said Lizzie. "I need to show it to someone at home first."

"As long as you turn it in tomorrow," said Miss Pennyroyal.

While her mother cooked dinner, Lizzie pulled Marvin into her lap.

"Listen to this," she said.

Lizzie gave Marvin a hug.

Big George lifted his chin and howled.

"That's only the beginning," said Lizzie. "Wait till you see what happens in Episode Two!"

STOP AND CHECK

Summarize Summarize what Lizzie did to write her comic book.

About the Author and Illustrator

Sarah Sullivan and her family moved a lot when she was growing up. She went to six different schools before she turned 8! In between moves, Sarah read lots of books and also made up her own stories, just like Lizzie. Now Sarah writes from her home in West Virginia, where you can find her with a pencil in her hand, making up stories.

Tricia Tusa announced that she wanted to write and illustrate children's books when she was just 5 years old. Today Tricia has illustrated more than 50 books by other authors. When she is given a book to illustrate, she reads the words first. Then she makes sketches quickly.

Author's Purpose

Sarah's story is about using imagination to write an adventure story. What can you learn from this story about getting ideas for your own writing?

Respond to the Text

Summarize

Use important details to summarize what happens in the story. Information from your Point of View chart may help you.

Character	Clue	Point of View

Write

How does the author use Lizzie's comic book to show how Lizzie feels about her brother? Use these sentence starters:

Before she writes her comic book, Lizzie feels…
The events in her comic book show…

Make Connections

How do brothers and sisters learn to get along? ESSENTIAL QUESTION

What are some things you have learned about getting along with others? TEXT TO WORLD

439

Compare Texts
Read about how students work together to stop bullying.

Bully-Free Zone

No one likes to be bullied. Bullying is when one person picks on or hurts another person. Sometimes a bully teases or calls someone names. A bully might not let someone join activities. Bullying can also be pushing or hitting.

Children from Seattle elementary schools worked together to stop bullying on the playground.

Elementary school students in Seattle, Washington, learned new tools to stop bullying. Everyone in the school community worked together. Students, teachers, parents, and school workers all participated.

During class, students learned how to be good friends and **cooperate** with others. Students learned what to do if they saw bullying interactions like teasing or someone being excluded.

The students practiced speaking up if they saw bullying. They learned to be a friend to someone who is bullied. They helped the person walk away. Each week, they had meetings to talk about bullying problems.

Soon there was less bullying at Seattle schools. Students didn't name-call on the playground. They didn't pick on others as much. School was more fun and safe for everyone. The program was a success!

Texas elementary school students learn about bullying in an after-school program.

Make Connections

How did children in Seattle schools learn to **interact** better? ESSENTIAL QUESTION

What have you read this week about how people get along? TEXT TO TEXT

Essential Question
What do heroes do?
Read about the brave woman who became the first African American female pilot.

Go Digital!

Brave Bessie

written and illustrated by
Eric Velasquez

Twice a year a library wagon would stop in front of Bessie Coleman's little house in Texas. Bessie's mom would rent books for her twelve children to read. Bessie loved to read about Booker T. Washington and Harriet Tubman. They were her heroes. Bessie daydreamed of being someone special like them.

Bessie knew school was important. She walked four miles each day to get to school, and four miles home. She practiced reading to her little brothers and sisters. She practiced her numbers by checking the money her family got for picking cotton.

Bessie scrimped and saved enough so she could go to college. She went to college at eighteen but left after only a few months. She could not afford to stay in school. But Bessie was not ready to give up on her dreams.

She decided to move to Chicago. Her brothers Walter and John lived there. It was a big and exciting city where people's dreams came true.

STOP AND CHECK

Summarize Summarize what Bessie did to prepare for college.

Bessie soon got a job in a barbershop. Bessie enjoyed listening to John tell stories about French lady pilots in World War I. Bessie had never heard of a lady pilot. The more Bessie thought, the more she liked the idea. Bessie knew she could learn to fly, too.

Bessie quickly **discovered** how hard it would be to become a pilot. In the 1920s, there were rules about who could learn to fly. Most people wouldn't teach someone with Bessie's skin color how to fly. Bessie did not **agree** with the rules, but she could not find anyone to teach her to fly.

445

One day Bessie met a very important man who worked at a newspaper. She asked him if he knew anyone that could teach her how to fly a plane. He told Bessie to go to France. That is where she had first heard of lady pilots! He told her it would be a lot of work, but Bessie was determined to **succeed**. She took classes and learned to speak French. She saved her money and was finally able to buy a ticket to France.

Bessie sailed to France on a steam ship. She had never been on a ship before. It was big and noisy. The ocean was windy and rough. Bessie was a little scared being on a big ship all by herself. She reminded herself that she was on her way to being somebody special. The trip took nine long days to sail across the Atlantic Ocean. Bessie stared out at the water, waiting to see land.

Finally, Bessie reached France. Soon she found a school that would teach her how to fly a plane. After years of hard work, Bessie was ready for her first flying lesson.

First Bessie had to **study** how to inspect a plane. This plane had wings made of wood and cloth. Bessie had to check the cloth wings for any tears. She also had to check the propeller.

After a few lessons, Bessie climbed into the back of the plane and her teacher climbed into the front. The propeller whirled and the engine chugged. After a running start, the plane took off. Bessie gripped the controls as she took to the air. Her cheeks were stinging from the cold wind, but Bessie was grinning.

Bessie had to walk miles and miles to the flying school each day, just like she walked to school as a child. Bessie practiced how to take off and how to land. She learned all the words for planes and flying—in English and in French.

Finally, Bessie became the first African-American woman to earn a pilot's license. People could call her an *aviatrix*, the name for a lady pilot. That meant she was truly someone special.

Pilot's License
Issued to: *Bessie Coleman*
Date issued: *15 June 1921*
Signature of Pilot
Bessie Coleman
License No. *18.310*

STOP AND CHECK

Summarize Bessie worked for years to earn her pilot's license. Summarize what she did to earn it.

449

Bessie returned to America. She was surprised to see reporters waiting to ask her questions. Many people were **interested** in Bessie. They wanted to see her fly her planes.

Bessie wanted to help other African Americans. She wanted children to know they could make their dreams come true. She decided to earn money for her own flying school by performing stunt-flying shows.

One sunny day, over one-thousand people paid to see Bessie **perform** in New York. The crowd cheered as Bessie climbed into the cockpit. She was wearing a leather coat, a helmet, goggles, and a confident smile.

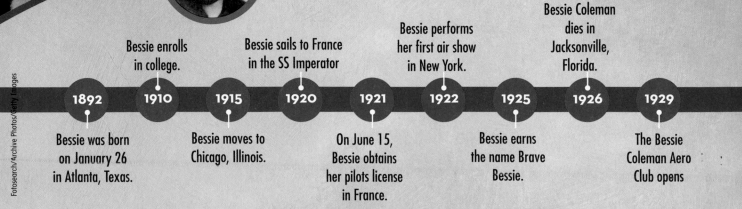

Brave Bessie

Bessie enrolls in college.

Bessie sails to France in the SS Imperator

Bessie performs her first air show in New York.

Bessie Coleman dies in Jacksonville, Florida.

| 1892 | 1910 | 1915 | 1920 | 1921 | 1922 | 1925 | 1926 | 1929 |

Bessie was born on January 26 in Atlanta, Texas.

Bessie moves to Chicago, Illinois.

On June 15, Bessie obtains her pilots license in France.

Bessie earns the name Brave Bessie.

The Bessie Coleman Aero Club opens

450

The plane slowly rolled down the field and took off. Bessie performed **challenging** flying stunts like figure eights and tailspins. The crowd went wild.

Bessie performed her stunts in Texas, Tennessee, and Illinois. She flew over fields like the one she picked cotton in as a child. Crowds of people were below her, waving and cheering. She had earned the title "Brave Bessie."

Years later, her dream of opening a school finally came true. The Bessie Coleman Aero Club taught African-American people how to fly. Thanks to Bessie, their dreams were taking flight, too.

About the Author and Illustrator

Eric Velasquez loved to draw when he was a child. As a grown-up, he has illustrated more than 300 books. For *Brave Bessie,* Eric made the illustrations and wrote the story, too. Bessie Coleman's story means a lot to Eric because she is an African American hero. That is why he wanted to tell her story to readers.

Eric often uses oil paints, pastels, and charcoal for his illustrations. If kids would like to do what Eric does when they grow up, he tells them to "draw, draw, draw, paint, paint, paint, read, read, read."

Author's Purpose

Eric includes a time line with the story. How does the time line help you understand Bessie Coleman's life?

Respond to the Text

Summarize

Use important details to summarize what happens in the selection. Information from your Sequence chart may help you.

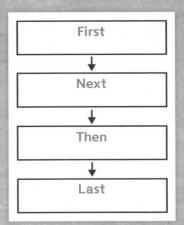

Write

How does the author use Bessie's story to show what it means to be a hero? Use these sentence starters:

The author starts by telling about...
The author shows Bessie's bravery by...

Make Connections

What did hero Bessie Coleman do? ESSENTIAL QUESTION

Bessie was brave to do what she did. What other brave things do heroes do? TEXT TO WORLD

Genre • Legend

Compare Texts
Read about a real girl who saved the lives of hundreds of people.

The Legend of Kate Shelley

One night many years ago, Kate Shelley woke up during a strong storm. She heard a familiar sound. It was the whistle of the Number 12 train. Kate knew the four people onboard were checking the bridge to see if it was safe for the midnight train to cross.

Kate Shelley

Kate heard the whistle again. Then she heard a crash and the hiss of steam. Kate ran to the bridge to **discover** it had broken. The Number 12 had crashed into the river far below. Kate knew she had to find a way to stop the midnight train because the engineer would not know the bridge was out.

The time line tells important events in Kate's life.

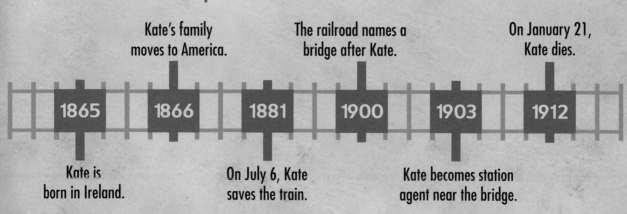

Kate's family moves to America.

The railroad names a bridge after Kate.

On January 21, Kate dies.

1865 1866 1881 1900 1903 1912

Kate is born in Ireland.

On July 6, Kate saves the train.

Kate becomes station agent near the bridge.

She had to get across the river somehow to warn the train. On hands and knees, Kate crawled across what was left of the bridge. Wind blew fiercely, and rain pelted her body. She could see the men from the Number 12 down below. Kate bravely kept crawling. Finally, Kate reached the other side of the river. She ran as fast as she could to the station.

Kate told the station agent what happened. They ran out to the railroad tracks and shone a red light toward the midnight train. It stopped just in time. Kate and the station agent were **heroes** because their bravery saved lives.

Make Connections

What did hero Kate Shelley do? ESSENTIAL QUESTION

How did all the heroes you have read about this week help their communities? TEXT TO TEXT

The Woodcutter's Gift

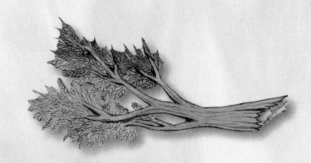

By Lupe Ruiz-Flores

Illustrations by Elaine Jerome

? Essential Question

How can we protect the Earth?

Read about a woodcutter who puts a tree to good use.

Go Digital!

On a stormy night, a violent thunderstorm blew
in and knocked down the giant mesquite tree
that stood in the town square. After the storm, all
the neighbors, who **rarely** spoke to each other,
came out of their houses and gathered around the
enormous tree that was blocking the main street.

"That tree is dead. Let's get rid of it," remarked the storekeeper as he poked at it with a stick. He looked up to see what the others thought.

The crowd muttered in agreement.

"Yeah," said the house painter. "I'll bring my saw and cut it into little pieces."

"No. Wait," the gardener said. "Let's ask the woodcutter Tomás what he thinks we should do."

"Tomás," said the gardener, "what should we do with this tree?"

"This rough and ugly mesquite is only good for one thing: firewood," said the grumpy painter.

"No, no," the woodcutter said, moving closer to the tree. "Don't destroy this good tree."

"What are you going to do with it?" the crowd asked.

The woodcutter paused, deep in thought. "This tree *could* belong to everyone."

"How can one tree belong to everyone? Not possible."

The woodcutter just grinned and replied, "It's a surprise. You'll see."

STOP AND CHECK

Make Predictions What do you think the woodcutter's surprise will be? Use the Make Predictions strategy to predict what he will do.

The next day the neighbors watched from a **distance** as the woodcutter split the tree into huge blocks. Then the men helped him haul the large pieces to his home.

Day after day, the townspeople watched as woodchips flew into the air like sparks from a fire as the woodcutter carved and chipped and whittled the wood.

"My dad says that ugly mesquite is only good for barbecues," one young boy said as he watched from the other side of the fence.

"Ah, but he's wrong," the woodcutter replied. "The beauty of this tree is not on the outside but on the inside."

Every day the **curious** neighbors went to watch the woodcutter work. They talked and laughed and wondered what he was doing.

"What are you making?" they kept asking him.

"Be patient," he would say and continue with his work.

One day, the woodcutter moved the chunks of wood inside his woodshed. Children peeked through the knotholes in the wall, but they couldn't see anything. The woodcutter worked every day until the sun went down. And every night, he locked the shed.

Finally, the woodcutter rang the big, rusty bell hanging on his porch. He had never done that before.

CLANG! CLANG! CLANG!

Everyone rushed over and gathered outside the woodcutter's house.

"What's happening? Why is the bell ringing?" they asked.

"Follow me," the woodcutter said, and he led them to the woodshed. "Now close your eyes and don't open them until I tell you."

The big woodshed door swung open. CREEEAAAK.

"Open your eyes now," the woodcutter said with joy. The townspeople opened their eyes and gasped.

"You see? I made a zoo for the children to enjoy," the woodcutter said **proudly**.

Life-sized wooden animals stood before them inside the shed.

"Wow! Yeah! Hurray!" the children shouted as they jumped up and down with excitement.

465

"This is a giraffe," squealed one little girl in delight as she stroked the giraffe's long neck.

"And there's a zebra over there," said another girl.

"Look, a lion and a tiger," one boy said as he ran his hand across the lion's mane.

"A turtle!" a little girl cheered as she counted the squares on the turtle's shell.

Even the painter couldn't believe his eyes. "Tomás created a spectacular zoo from that dried-up old mesquite tree."

STOP AND CHECK

Summarize What did the woodcutter do to make the zoo? Summarize how he made the tree into his surprise.

Everyone helped carry the animals one by one to the town square.

"These animals still need a coat of paint," the woodcutter said. "They're not finished yet."

"Can we paint them?" the children begged as they circled around the woodcutter.

"Of course," he replied, scratching his head, "as soon as I get some paint."

"Wait. We'll get the paint," said the neighbors, rushing home. They returned with an odd assortment of leftover paint and paintbrushes.

67

Everyone gathered in the square to paint the animals. When they finally finished, they giggled at the orange giraffe with the brown spots, cherry red lips, long black eyelashes, and bright blue hooves. They laughed at the turtle with the pink and green squares on its shell. They pointed to the yellow and purple stripes on the zebra.

"I couldn't have done a better job myself," said the woodcutter, smiling.

To celebrate, the townspeople had a big party in the square. The adults watched the children play in the zoo. They painted brightly colored booths and decorated them with giant paper flowers in red, blue, green, yellow, and purple. Everyone enjoyed snow cones in rainbow colors.

A few days later, men dressed in suits and ties came to talk to the woodcutter. The curious neighbors gathered outside his house. A short while later, the woodcutter came out and addressed the crowd.

"These gentlemen from the city want to buy the zoo for the museum. They say it's a work of art," he said, smiling sheepishly. Tomás had never thought of himself as an artist.

Everyone was quiet. Then a little boy asked sadly, "Does that mean we'll lose our zoo?"

The children were ready to cry. Would their zoo be taken away?

The woodcutter looked at the crowd. "Look at how our zoo has brought us all together," he told the men in suits. "The zoo belongs here. It's not for sale. But I will donate one piece to the museum so others can enjoy it, too."

All the people cheered. The children jumped up and down. Everyone formed a circle around the woodcutter. They celebrated. They danced.

By the time it got dark, everyone was exhausted. That night, the children slept so soundly that they did not see Mr. Giraffe stretch his long neck and snap a leaf from the tree. They did not catch Mr. Lion's curly mane blowing **gently** in the breeze as he yawned. They missed seeing Mr. Zebra's purple and yellow stripes swirl as he pranced around the yard. And no one saw Mr. Tiger's tail swish back and forth as he swatted a fly. No, no one saw the special magic that filled the air that night. They were just happy knowing that the woodcutter's gift would still be there in the morning.

About the Author and Illustrator

Lupe Ruiz-Flores lives in Texas where mesquite trees grow. She got the idea for *The Woodcutter's Gift* from two articles she read in a newspaper. One article was about a real woodcutter, and the other was about a Mexican folk artist. Lupe learned storytelling from her father and grandmother. She tells stories in Spanish and English.

Elaine Jerome started illustrating little paper books as soon as she could hold a crayon. She studied animals and plants at an art school. That inspired the colorful ones she drew for *The Woodcutter's Gift*.

Author's Purpose

In the first part of the story, Lupe keeps you guessing about what the woodcutter is doing. Why do you think she does this?

Respond to the Text

Summarize

Use important details to summarize what happens in the story. Information from your Problem and Solution chart may help you.

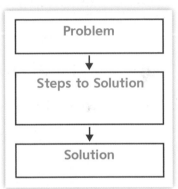

Write

How does the author help you understand the message of the story? Use these sentence starters:

The characters' words show...
The characters' actions show...

Make Connections

How did the woodcutter help protect the Earth? **ESSENTIAL QUESTION**

What is something you learned about gifts from reading this story? **TEXT TO WORLD**

Compare Texts
Read about rock and mineral resources and how we can protect them.

Earth's Resources

What is above, below, and all around Earth? **Earth resources**! Go outdoors. You'll feel a gentle breeze move across your face or a strong wind blow. Look below. You are stepping on soil and rocks. Listen for the gush of a gentle stream or the thunder of ocean waves. Earth resources are materials from Earth that people use in daily life. Air, wind, water, rocks, and soil are all natural resources. We use them everyday.

Rocks and Minerals

Rocks and minerals are everywhere. Look for them in the ground, sand, water, or ice. Rocks can be big or little, rough or smooth. Have you seen a rock that sparkled? Some rocks shine because of the minerals they contain. Like rocks, minerals are not alive. Minerals can be different shapes, sizes, and colors. As rocks and minerals break down, they form soil. Here are how some rocks and minerals look and feel.

Rocks and Minerals

Igneous Rocks	**Basalt**	Basalt is dark black. Sometimes it has gas bubbles inside.
Sedimentary Rocks	**Shale**	Shale can be black, red, brown, or blue. When it is wet, it smells like mud.
Metamorphic Rocks	**Marble**	Marble is a smooth multicolored rock. Sometimes it has shiny crystals.
Minerals	**Quartz**	Quartz is a hard mineral. It looks like glass.

We use rocks and minerals in many ways. We use granite to make buildings and monuments. We also use it in our kitchens to make countertops. We make statues out of marble. Many rocks are used to make tools. Minerals are used to make everything from our food to our cars.

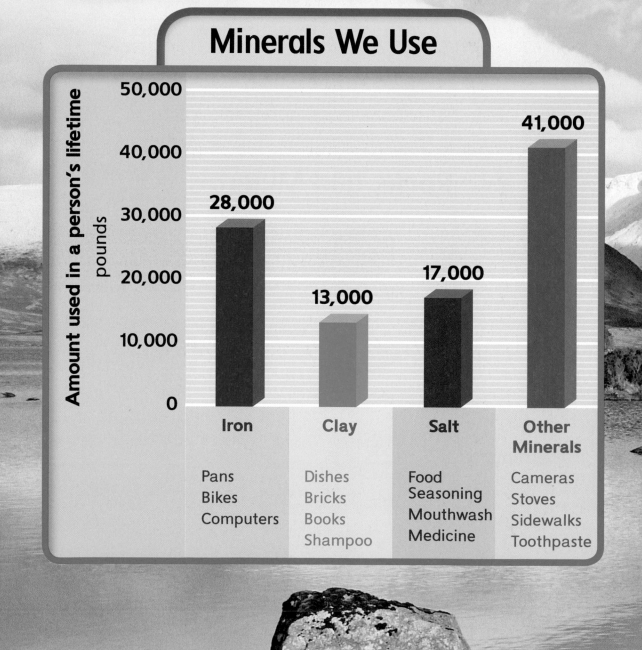

Minerals We Use

Amount used in a person's lifetime pounds

Iron	Clay	Salt	Other Minerals
28,000	13,000	17,000	41,000
Pans	Dishes	Food	Cameras
Bikes	Bricks	Seasoning	Stoves
Computers	Books	Mouthwash	Sidewalks
	Shampoo	Medicine	Toothpaste

Saving Our Resources

We have a good **supply** of some natural resources. The Earth replaces air and water quickly when we use them up. The Earth does not make more rocks and minerals as quickly. We can keep a good supply of Earth resources by reusing things we have. We can recycle things we no longer need.

These things help people reduce pollution and keep natural resources like water and soil clean. If people work together, Earth's resources will be here for everyone to use for a long time.

Make Connections

What can you do to protect Earth resources like rocks and minerals? **ESSENTIAL QUESTION**

What natural resources have you read about this week? **TEXT TO TEXT**

TIME
FOR KIDS®

Setting the Rules

Essential Question

Why are rules important?

Read about how the Constitution sets the rules for our country.

Go Digital!

The Framers met in Philadelphia to form the rules for our country.

Who came up with the rules for our country?

Your parents vote. You can say what you think about a new law. People in your neighborhood can have a meeting. You are free to believe whatever you want. You can thank the Constitution for all of these things.

In 1787, a group of men met in Philadelphia. They thought the country needed a better government because each state had its own **rules**. They wanted to create a **united** government that would work together. They decided to **form** a new set of rules called the Constitution. Everyone in the country would follow these rules.

Creating the Constitution

The **writers** of the Constitution included George Washington, Benjamin Franklin, James Madison, and other state leaders. They were called Framers because they framed, or planned, the rules.

STOP AND CHECK

Make Predictions How do you think the Framers formed the Constitution?

The Framers didn't always agree. They often **exclaimed** loudly that they would not sign the new rules and make them official. **Finally**, after four months of debate, the Framers agreed on the rules.

The Constitution is now the highest law of the United States. It explains the rules of the country and it tells how our government works. It gives rights, or privileges, to all the people.

The Constitution

The Constitution isn't just about our nation's past **history** or its current rules. The document has become a symbol. Like the American flag, it stands for freedom and liberty.

You can see the Constitution at the National Archives Building in Washington, D. C.

Adults have the right to vote. You have the right to say your ideas or express your opinions. We have the right to live safely in our homes. These rights are explained in the Constitution.

Changing with Time

Over time, the Constitution has changed. Some rules have been added to the original document to help make life better or safer for the **public**. The first ten rules added are called the Bill of Rights. They name the rights that belong to people in America. Another change gave women the right to vote. So far, there have been 27 changes to the Constitution. That's why it's known as a living document. It can be changed or updated at any time.

You can also see the Bill of Rights at the National Archives Building in Washington, D. C.

Respond to the Text

1. Use details to summarize the selection. SUMMARIZE

2. How does the way the author organizes the information help you understand the Constitution? WRITE

3. Why are a country's rules important? ESSENTIAL QUESTION

4. Why is it important to have one set of rules for the entire country? TEXT TO WORLD

Compare Texts

Read about where you can find American symbols today.

American Symbols

When you think of the United States, what image comes to mind? Do you picture the Statue of Liberty? How about the White House? These buildings and other important places and papers are national symbols. Here's a look at some famous symbols. Can you think of others?

White House

The White House has been the home for every U.S. president except George Washington. He laid the first stone, but the first president to move in was John Adams. The White House has become a symbol of the American president.

Liberty Bell

The Liberty Bell was originally ordered as a bell for Independence Hall. That is where the people who formed the Constitution met. The crack in the bell is more than two feet long! Just like its name, the bell symbolizes liberty.

New York

Philadelphia

Washington D. C. ★

Statue of Liberty

The Statue of Liberty was a gift from France for the 100 year anniversary of the Declaration of Independence. But there wasn't enough money to complete it in time. The statue was not put up until 10 years after the anniversary. It is a symbol of freedom and hope.

Constitution

The Constitution is a document that tells the rights and rules of people who live in the United States. It is kept under special glass in a building that is home to many famous documents. The Constitution stands for freedom and liberty.

N
W ← ⊙ → E
S

Make Connections

Why are the **rules** in the Constitution important? ESSENTIAL QUESTION

What are some important American symbols? TEXT TO TEXT

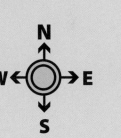

Key

United States

★ National Capital

● Cities

THE GOLDEN FLOWER

A TAINO MYTH FROM PUERTO RICO

By Nina Jaffe

Illustrated by Enrique O. Sánchez

Essential Question

What do myths help us understand?

Read a myth about how a golden flower grows.

Go Digital!

In the beginning of the world, there was no
water anywhere on earth. There was only a tall
mountain that stood alone on a wide desert plain.

There were no green plants. There were
no flowers. All the people lived on top of this
mountain.

One day, a child went walking on the dry land
below the mountain. As he bent down over the
ground looking for food, something floated by
on the wind. He reached out and caught it in his
hand. It was a seed. A small, brown seed. He put
the seed into his pouch.

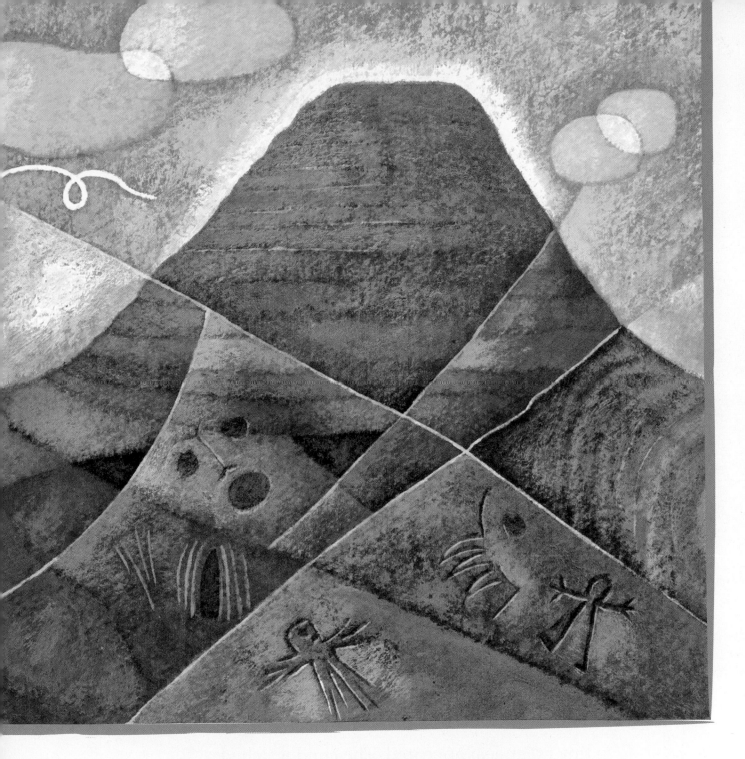

The next day, he went walking, and again found something as it floated by on the wind. It was another seed. Day by day, he gathered these seeds until his pouch was full. It could not hold anymore. And the child said to himself, "I will plant these seeds at the top of our mountain."

He planted the seeds and waited. One morning,
a tiny green leaf appeared. The child watched.
From under the ground, a forest began to grow
high on top of the mountain.

All the people came to see. It was a forest of
many-colored flowers, a magic garden of green
leaves and thick branches. The child was happy.

492

In the middle of the forest, at the foot of the
tallest tree, there grew a vine that wrapped itself
around the tree.

And from that vine
there grew a flower more
beautiful than all the
rest. A bright flower with
golden petals.

STOP AND CHECK

Reread What happened
after the child planted the
seeds? Reread to check your
understanding.

And from that flower, something new
appeared in the forest. It looked like a little ball.
"Look!" cried the child. "Something is growing
out of the flower!"

As the people gathered around to watch, the
ball grew larger and larger, until it became a great
yellow globe that shone like the sun. Even as they
walked on the dry land far below, people could
see it **shining** on top of the mountain.

One woman said, "If you put your ear next to the ball, you can hear strange noises coming from inside." The people listened. Strange sounds and murmuring could be heard. But nobody knew what was hidden inside.

The people were afraid. After that, they all stayed away. Even the child stayed away.

One day, a man walking on the desert plain saw the golden ball. He said, "If that shining ball were mine, I would have the power of the sun. I could light up the sky, or make darkness fall." And he ran toward it, climbing up the rocky mountainside.

On the other side of the mountain, another man
saw the shining globe, and he also said, "I want that
thing for myself. It will give me great powers." He,
too, began to run. Each one climbed quickly. Each
one found a footpath that led to the tree.

They both ran without stopping until they
reached the shining globe at the same time. But
what they found was not really a ball; it was the
fruit of the golden flower: a *calabaza*—a pumpkin.

The two men began to fight and argue.

"It is mine!" said one.

"No, it is mine!" said the other.

Each man grabbed the pumpkin. They pushed and pulled. They pulled and tugged until . . .

. . . finally, the vine broke. The pumpkin began to roll down the mountain faster and faster, until it crashed into a sharp rock and burst apart.

Whoosh! Waves of water poured out of the pumpkin. The water bubbled and foamed. The waves began to cover the earth, flooding the desert plain, rising higher and higher.

For it was the sea that had been hidden inside the pumpkin. Out came the creatures: whales, dolphins, crabs, and sunfish. All the people ran to the top of the mountain to hide in the forest of green leaves.

STOP AND CHECK

Make Predictions What do you think will happen after the people run to the top of the mountain? Use the Make Predictions strategy to predict what happens next.

"Will the whole earth be covered?" they cried.

Higher and higher the waters kept rising, up the sides of the mountain.

But when the water reached the **edge** of the magic forest the little boy had planted, it stopped.

The people peeked out from behind the leaves. And what did they see? Small streams running through the trees. A beach of golden sand. And the wide open ocean, sparkling all around them.

Now the people could drink from the cool streams and splash in the rippling waves. Now they could gather fish from the flowing tides and plant their **crops**.

The child laughed and sang as the sun shone
down and breezes blew through the green leaves
and **rustled** the many-colored flowers. Water
had come to the earth!

And that is how, the Taino say, between
the sun and the sparkling blue sea, their island
home—Boriquén—came to be.

ABOUT THE
AUTHOR AND ILLUSTRATOR

Nina Jaffe loved reading ancient myths and folktales as a child. She started retelling them to her friends. She liked retelling old stories so much that she still does today, as an author. Nina has traveled to Puerto Rico and many other places around the world to study storytelling.

Enrique O. Sánchez grew up in the Dominican Republic, not far from Puerto Rico. He moved to the United States and started making art. He painted signs and scenery for plays. He even made art for television shows. Now he is a painter and an illustrator of picture books.

AUTHOR'S PURPOSE

As Nina retells the myth, she imagines what the ancient people might say. Why do you think she includes *dialogue*, the words people in the story say?

Respond to the Text

Summarize

Use important details to summarize what happens in the selection. Information from your Theme chart may help you.

Clue
↓
Clue
↓
Clue
↓
Theme

Write

How does the author help you to understand that the world changed from the beginning to the end of the story?

> The author uses illustrations...
> At the beginning of the story, the land was...
> At the end of the story, the land was...

Make Connections

What does this myth help you understand about pumpkin plants?
ESSENTIAL QUESTION

What is something you learned about Puerto Rico from this myth?
TEXT TO WORLD

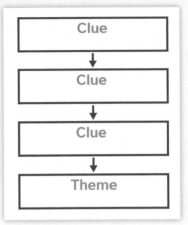

Compare Texts
Read about how a pumpkin
plant grows and develops.

A Pumpkin Plant

Pumpkins are a familiar sight each fall.
Some people decorate them, some bake
pumpkin pie, and others eat the seeds.
Have you ever seen a pumpkin grow
and **develop** from a seed? Let's learn
about this amazing process.

Inside a Pumpkin

If you have ever watched someone
carve a pumpkin, you know that there
are a lot of seeds inside. All pumpkins
begin as seeds. If you plant the seed in
soil, and give it the water, light, and
air it needs, it will become a new
pumpkin plant.

Pumpkins contain
many seeds.

Seed
Coat

Seed
Food

Tiny
Plant

Inside the seed is
everything needed to
grow a new pumpkin
plant.

Pumpkin Plant

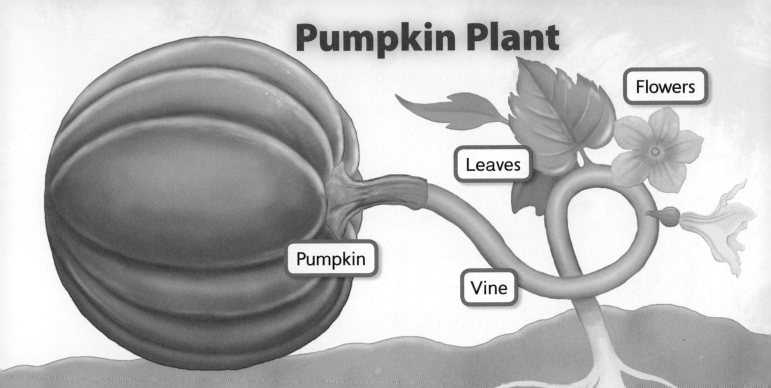

Flowers

Leaves

Pumpkin

Vine

Roots

How to Grow Pumpkins

Plant seeds in a sunny place.

Plant them in the spring.

1. Form soil into a small mound.

2. Place 4 to 5 seeds in the top of the mound.

3. Water the seeds.

4. Keep the soil moist.

You will see sprouts in 1 to 2 weeks.

Pumpkins will be ready in about 4 months.

You have seen a tiny pumpkin seed and a grown-up pumpkin plant. Now let's learn about the **stages** in between.

A Seed Grows

You plant a pumpkin seed and give it water. In a few days, you will see a small, green sprout above the ground. At the same time, roots grow below the ground.

Each day, the sprout grows. When it is long, it is called a vine. The vine continues to grow longer, spreading out along the ground. Yellow flowers, which will become pumpkins, appear on the vine.

Small, green pumpkins grow where the flowers were. Over time, the pumpkins get bigger and turn orange. Soon they are ready to be picked. Now the cycle can begin again.

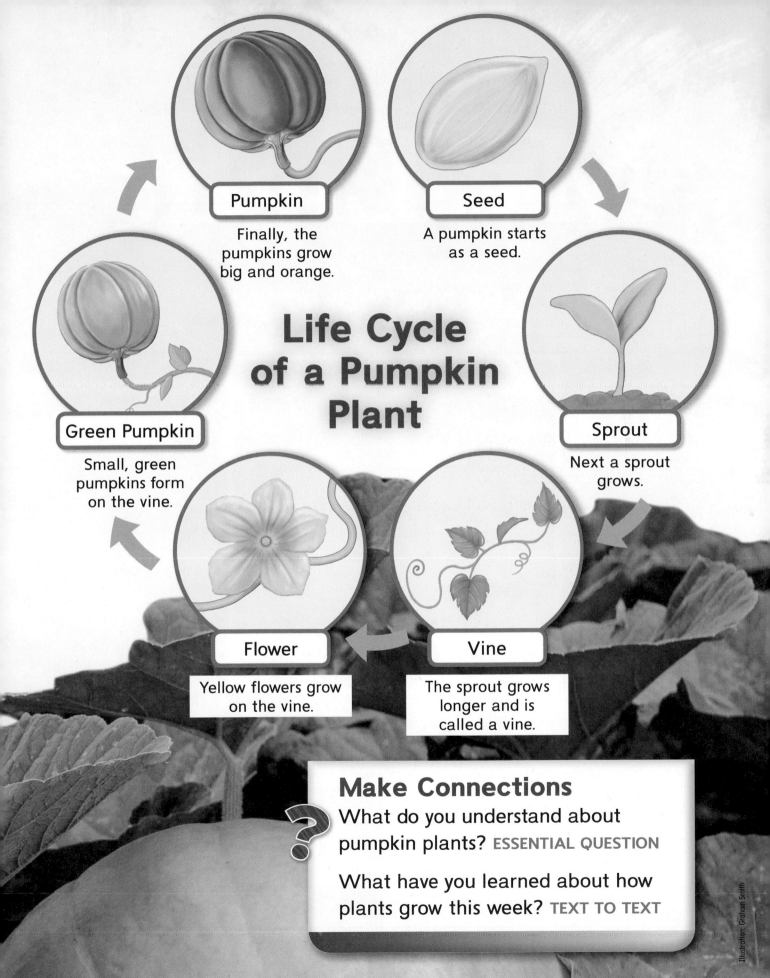

Pumpkin

Finally, the pumpkins grow big and orange.

Seed

A pumpkin starts as a seed.

Life Cycle of a Pumpkin Plant

Green Pumpkin

Small, green pumpkins form on the vine.

Sprout

Next a sprout grows.

Flower

Yellow flowers grow on the vine.

Vine

The sprout grows longer and is called a vine.

Make Connections

What do you understand about pumpkin plants? ESSENTIAL QUESTION

What have you learned about how plants grow this week? TEXT TO TEXT

Illustration: Graham Smith

511

My Light

BY MOLLY BANG

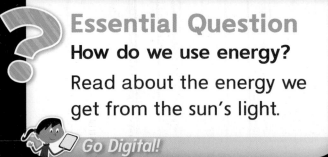

Essential Question

How do we use energy?

Read about the energy we get from the sun's light.

Go Digital!

When you see the city lights at night, they look like stars have fallen down to earth.

Those lights ARE starlight—my light.

I am your sun, a golden star.

You see my radiance as light.

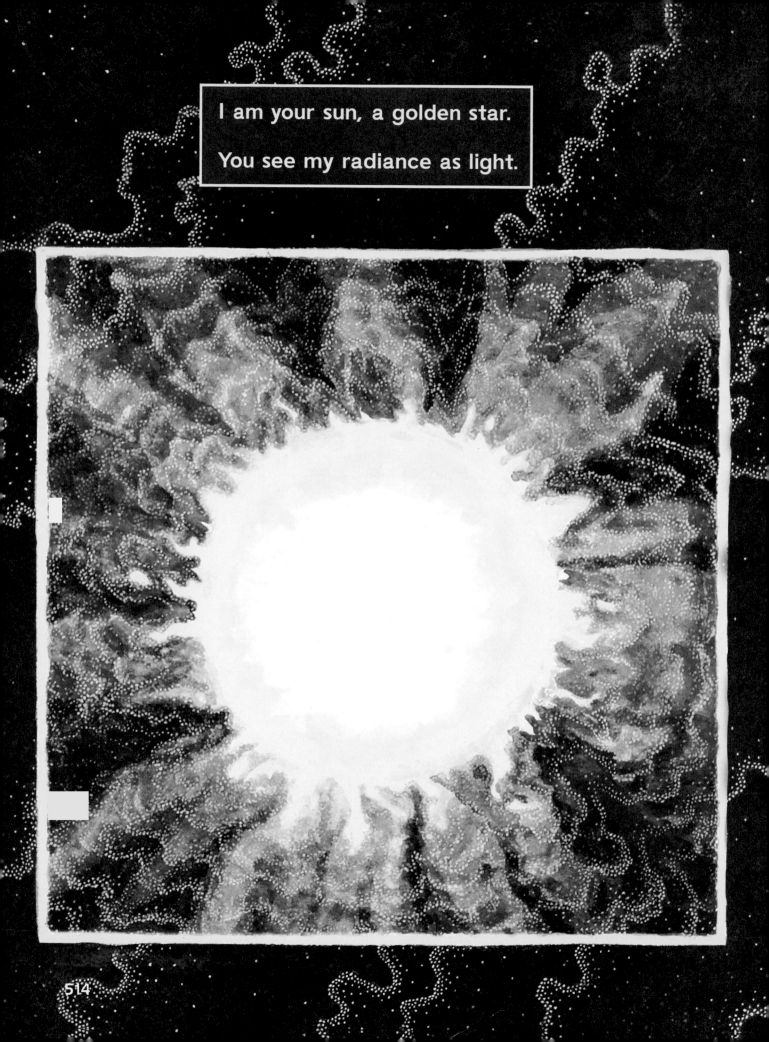

Each day I warm your
land and water.

Tiny drops of warm water
rise and form clouds.

515

The clouds cool down.

My **energy** falls in rain.

The water **flows** from streams to
rivers, carrying my energy

down,

down,

down.

A dam! You humans stop the flow. My energy is trapped.

Whish! Some water shoots down tunnels to giant turbines.

Whoosh! The water spins the turbines round and round. It spins my energy to generators, which make **electricity.**

Now my energy is in the electricity. It flows away in copper wires.

STOP AND CHECK

Reread What happens after the dam traps the energy? Reread to check your understanding.

The wires hum!
Electricity flows,
pulsing, pulsing, pulsing
my energy out
to your towns
and cities.

Each day I shine on earth and warm the air. The warm air rises. Cooler air pours in and makes the wind.

Swish! Swoosh! The wind pushes blades of turbines round and round, spinning my energy to generators, which make electricity.

Electricity pours into copper wires and flows out to your towns and cities.

Green plants catch my light
and use my energy to help
build leaves and stems.

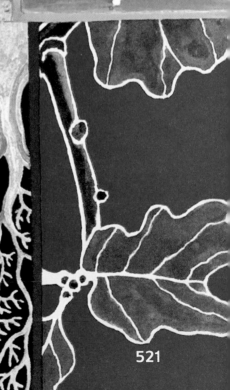

My energy builds each bush and flower, reed and cactus, fruit and tree. My light fuels all the plants on earth.

Some of the plants are eaten. My energy flows to everything that eats them.

Other plants die and are buried. Some were buried millions and millions of years ago and turned to coal. Then my energy stayed deep **underground**, locked inside the coal.

Crunch! Roar! Now you humans dig up the coal. You **haul** it out and burn it.

The fire heats water into steam. Whoosh! The steam shoots against giant turbines, which spin round and round. They send my energy to generators, which make electricity.

From coal-fired **power** plants, electricity flows in copper wires, out to your towns and cities.

My light falls on **solar** cells and charges their electrons.

No turbines, no generators—electricity streams across the cells, which pour it into copper wires.

Electricity flows to the building below.

When darkness falls, you turn a switch.

From rushing wind and water, from burning coal, from **silent** solar cells, you let my energy into your room.

Electricity lights the night.

Inside a light bulb, a wire grows hot. It glows.

Inside a fluorescent tube, gas is energized. It glows.

When you turn on lights at night, they look like stars have fallen down to earth.

Those lights are energy from me, your golden star, caught and transformed by your earth, and by yourselves.

For a moment, my light illuminates your towns and cities.

Then, like the starlight from which it came, it fades back into space.

STOP AND CHECK

Reread How does the Sun's light illuminate your town? Reread to check your understanding.

About the Author and Illustrator

Molly Bang grew up surrounded by science because both of her parents were scientists. Molly spent summers at Science School and visited the labs in which her parents worked.

Today Molly is an award-winning author and illustrator. She writes lively words and creates colorful pictures to explain or to tell a story. Molly has won a Caldecott Honor three times for her illustrations.

Author's Purpose

Molly has the Sun speak and tell about electricity. When an author makes something act or be like a person, it is called *personification*. In real life, the Sun cannot tell a story. Why do you think Molly gives the information in this way?

Respond to the Text

Summarize

Use important details to summarize what happens in the selection. Information from your Author's Purpose chart may help you.

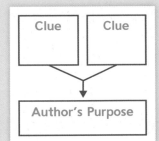

Write

How does repeating the words "my light" help you understand how we use energy? Use these sentence starters:

> The words "my light" mean...
> We use energy from the Sun's light to...

Make Connections

How do we use energy to make electricity?
ESSENTIAL QUESTION

What kinds of energy do people use where you live?
TEXT TO WORLD

Compare Texts
Read about the water cycle and
how people use water energy.

THE POWER OF WATER

Do you know what happens when it rains?
Raindrops fall from clouds in the sky. Then the
rainstorm passes away, but it leaves behind
puddles of water on the ground. Soon the
puddles disappear, too. What has happened to
the water? Is it gone for good?

The water does not disappear. Earth's water
is always being recycled. Water is continuously
moving on, above and below Earth's surface.
This process is called the *water cycle*.

Markus Botzek/Zinnium/age fotostock

THE WATER CYCLE

The warmth of the Sun heats up the water on Earth's surface. This **solar** energy changes the liquid water into a gas called *water vapor*. Water vapor rises into the air and turns into liquid drops of water that form clouds.

When the water gets heavy in the clouds, it falls back to Earth as rain. In cold temperatures, it may fall as snow, sleet, or hail, which are solid forms of water.

The falling water refills rivers, lakes, and oceans. That's why it's called a water cycle— because the same events happen over and over in the same order. There is no beginning and no end, just like a circle.

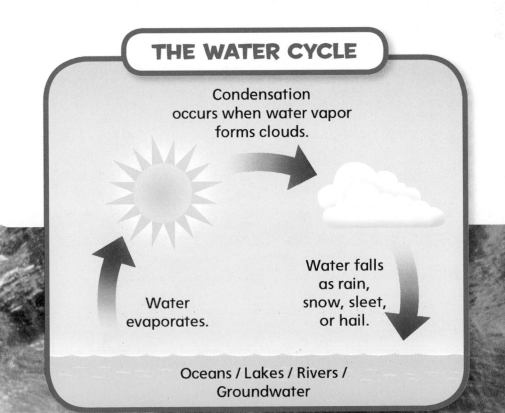

THE WATER CYCLE

Condensation occurs when water vapor forms clouds.

Water evaporates.

Water falls as rain, snow, sleet, or hail.

Oceans / Lakes / Rivers / Groundwater

ENERGY FROM WATER

Water is one source of **power** that people use. Power, or energy, is the ability to do work. When water moves fast, it carries energy. A fast-flowing river is one example of moving water. The water is powerful enough to push not only people in rafts but also rocks and trees. A waterfall, another example of moving water, carries energy, too. The higher the waterfall, the more energy it carries.

The power of water can move people in rafts.

PUTTING WATER TO WORK

People know how to put moving water to work. Waterpower is used to create electricity. First workers build a dam on a fast-flowing river. The dam holds back the river's flow. Workers control the amount of water that passes through it. Once inside the dam, the water moves through a pipe to make electricity. Then the electricity is delivered to people along power lines.

People depend on Earth's water cycle for their supply of water. Many people also depend on waterpower for their electricity.

The Glen Canyon Dam is built on the Colorado River.

Make Connections

How do people use water energy?
ESSENTIAL QUESTION

What are some ways to make energy that you have read about this week?
TEXT TO TEXT

(inset) Dennis M. Herzog/Flickr/Getty Images

ASTRONAUT HANDBOOK

MEGHAN MCCARTHY

Essential Question

Why is teamwork important?

Read about how teams of astronauts get ready to explore space.

Go Digital!

536

Welcome to astronaut school! Soon you will be boarding a space shuttle and BLASTING into outer space. All different kinds of people have become astronauts. There have been teachers, painters, and even deep-sea divers. You can be an astronaut, too!

First you need to decide what kind
of astronaut you will be.

There are astronauts who
fly the space shuttles . . .

astronauts who conduct
scientific experiments,
such as growing plants . . .

and astronauts who **repair** satellites.

Becoming an astronaut takes a lot of preparation. It's **important** to study hard in school. Studying isn't always easy, but stick with it!

You will have to pass some tough fitness tests to become an astronaut, so suit up and start swimming! One test is to swim in your flight suit and sneakers.

It's also important to be a team player. While in space, you'll be eating, sleeping, and working in very tight quarters with many other people, so be nice to your neighbor and no fighting!

Now that you can work well with others, it's time for survival training. This training will help toughen you up and **prepare** you to live in harsh conditions.

After you're both mentally and physically prepared, it's time for the real work to begin. Practice makes perfect. Those of you who have decided to become engineers will practice working with **machines** much like the ones you'll use in space.

STOP AND CHECK

Summarize Summarize what you have read about so far about an astronaut's preparation.

Those of you who want to be a pilot of the
space shuttle will need to learn how to fly.

You've done the hard stuff, and now it's time to have some fun! A special plane nicknamed the Vomit Comet will take you high in the sky and then ZOOM back down. As a **result**, you'll be able to FLOAT! It might upset your stomach, but you'll get the hang of it.

You'll also need to pick the food you'd like to eat while in space. It's important to have a balanced diet to stay strong during your trip. You can even have dessert, such as freeze-dried ice cream!

This is what a space toilet looks like.

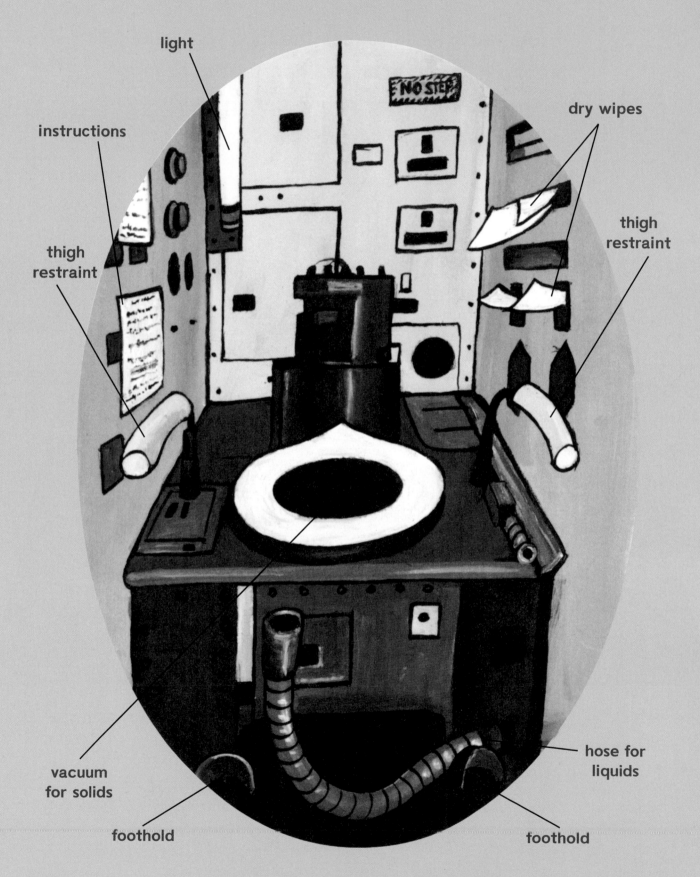

light

instructions

thigh restraint

dry wipes

thigh restraint

vacuum for solids

foothold

hose for liquids

foothold

And here's what your space suit will look like.

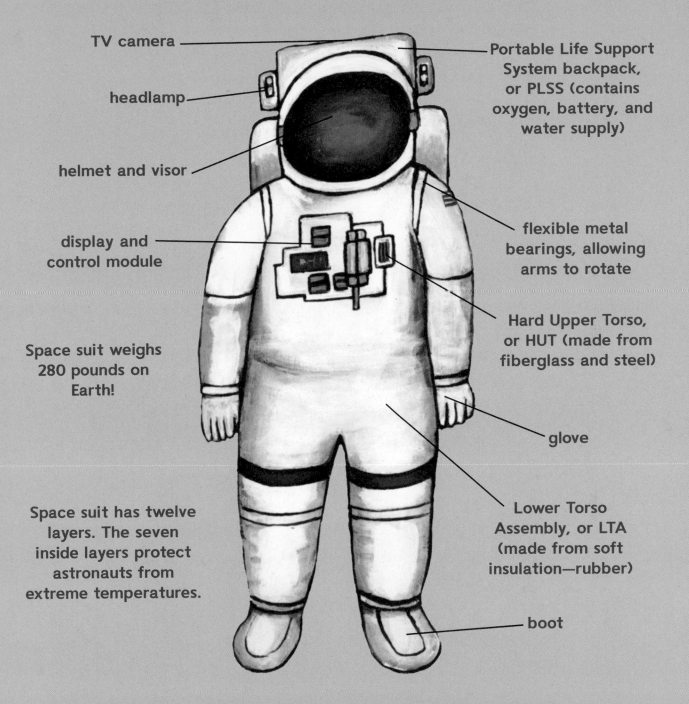

TV camera

headlamp

helmet and visor

display and
control module

Space suit weighs
280 pounds on
Earth!

Space suit has twelve
layers. The seven
inside layers protect
astronauts from
extreme temperatures.

Portable Life Support
System backpack,
or PLSS (contains
oxygen, battery, and
water supply)

flexible metal
bearings, allowing
arms to rotate

Hard Upper Torso,
or HUT (made from
fiberglass and steel)

glove

Lower Torso
Assembly, or LTA
(made from soft
insulation—rubber)

boot

You'll wear this suit while working outside the
space shuttle. It's white to reflect the rays of the
sun. It will be fitted to your exact measurements.
Over one hundred measurements will be taken of
your hand alone.

547

Finally it's time to blast off! Put on your orange flight suit, worn for takeoffs and landings, and get ready to board the space shuttle. You will have to sit for as long as three hours before liftoff.

Get ready for the
ride of your life.

3 . . . 2 . . . 1 . . .
BLASTOFF!

It's best to like small spaces.

551

ABOUT THE AUTHOR AND ILLUSTRATOR

MEGHAN MCCARTHY built a spaceship in her garage when she was six. She also played in a cardboard spaceship in her classroom. After Meghan grew up and became a writer, she wanted to write a book that would "not be like any space book out there for kids." She wanted to explain what astronauts actually go through to become astronauts.

Meghan has been illustrating books for a long time. She illustrated her first picture book before she even learned how to read! She drew the pictures first. Then she told her grandmother what to write down for the words.

AUTHOR'S PURPOSE

Meghan writes this selection as if she's talking to the reader. She uses the word *you*. Why do you think she writes this way?

Respond to the Text

Summarize

Use important details to summarize what happens in the selection. Information from your Main Idea and Key Details chart may help you.

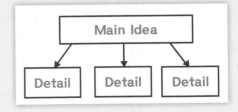

Write

How does the author make learning about an astronaut's job interesting? Use these sentence starters:

The author begins by...
She shares information by...
The illustrations make me...

Make Connections

Why is teamwork important for astronauts? **ESSENTIAL QUESTION**

How do members of your class work together as a team? **TEXT TO WORLD**

Genre • Expository Text

Compare Texts
Read about a team that climbed to the top of the world.

Teamwork to the Top

When Jordan Romero was nine, he saw a painting of the tallest mountains in the world. Jordan set a goal to climb each one, but he had a problem. He could not do it alone. Jordan knew what would solve his problem: a team to climb with him. His father and stepmother, experienced mountain climbers, became his teammates.

The Team Prepares

Before climbing, the team followed an exercise plan. They ran long distances while wearing heavy backpacks and pulling tires. They developed strong bodies to prepare them for the tough climb, while forming strong bonds that would help them work together.

At I3, Jordan Romero became the youngest person to climb Mt. Everest.

Getting to Everest

Jordan's team was ready for the dangers of **exploration**. Mt. Everest is the world's tallest mountain. The top of Mt. Everest is higher than some planes fly! At the top there is little oxygen to breathe, which is a problem for climbers. Lack of oxygen could make them sick, so the team solved the problem by wearing oxygen masks.

Jordan's team needed more help, so climbing experts called sherpas joined them. Each expert brought something special to the team.

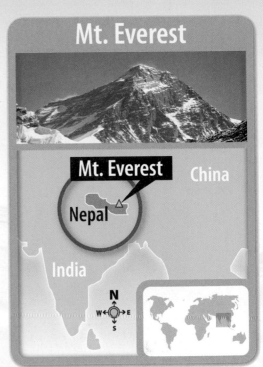

Reaching the Top

Team Jordan was on the mountain for 51 days. A rope linked the climbers together, and they worked together to stay safe. When they finally reached the summit, Jordan and his teammates celebrated. It was **teamwork** that helped them reach the tallest point in the world!

Make Connections

Why was teamwork important for Jordan's explorations? ESSENTIAL QUESTION

How do teams work together to solve problems? TEXT TO TEXT

MONEY MADNESS

by David A. Adler - illustrated by Edward Miller

Essential Question

How do we use money?

Read about how money works.

Go Digital!

What's all this **money** madness?
People talk about money and work for it.
They seem to always want more of it.
Take a look at a dollar bill.
There's a nice portrait of
George Washington on it,
but it's just paper!

SALE!
$$$$
SALE!
$$$$
SALE!

MONE
MADNES

100% WHOLE
WHEAT

VIDEO
GAME

Why do people want money? People want money because it can be used to buy things.

Now, imagine a world without money. If you were hungry and there was no such thing as money, how would you buy a loaf of bread? You would have to bake your own.

Without money, how would you get the ingredients for the bread? If no one would give or sell you flour, you would have to grow wheat, harvest it, grind it, and sift it before you would have flour for your bread.

If there was no such thing as money and you needed new clothes, you would have to make them.

Imagine if you had to knit your own sweater. Imagine if you had to raise a sheep and shear it, spin the wool to make yarn, and then knit the sweater yourself.

There was a time before money. Long ago, people couldn't buy things. When they were hungry, they gathered berries and killed animals. When they were cold, they gathered wood for their fires.

Before there was money, people gathered and hunted for what they needed. They were self-sufficient.

Some people liked to hunt. They were good at it. Others were good at making clubs or clothing. Soon people traded one thing for another. A hunter traded with a food gatherer. A club maker traded with a clothing maker.

A **system** of trading one thing for another is called bartering.

Maybe you barter. Have you ever traded one toy for another? At lunch, have you ever traded an apple for an orange? That's bartering.

However, there are times when bartering doesn't work. A hunter could trade an animal for berries, but how many berries? And what if the hunter didn't want berries?

How would a baker trade for a house? How many loaves of bread would he have to trade?

And why would anyone want so much bread? Long before a person could eat all that bread, most of it would be stale.

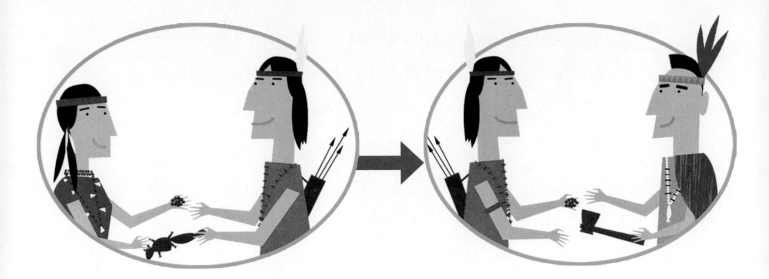

A hunter who didn't want berries might be willing to trade for them anyway if he knew he could then trade the berries for something he did want.

A home owner might be willing to trade her house for bread if she knew she could then trade the bread for something she did want.

In those trades, the berries and bread would be a kind of money.

At one time cows, sheep, camels, rocks, feathers, salt, dried fish, fishhooks, animal skins and strings of beads made from clamshells were all used as money.

People **valued** cows, sheep, and camels. And they could always trade one of those animals for something they wanted.

But what if something was **worth** just half a cow? You wouldn't want to cut a cow in half to buy something.

What if the sheep or camel you wanted to trade was sickly? You might have trouble trading it.

When animals were used as money, your money needed to be fed. Your money could die. It could run away.

Rocks were another early form of money. Rocks come in different sizes, but they're heavy to carry around.

Feathers were used as money too. Feathers are light, but they can blow away.

What was needed was something that wouldn't get sick, didn't have to be fed, wasn't too heavy or light, came in different weights or sizes, and most people wanted.

STOP AND CHECK

Summarize Summarize the early forms of money that you have read about.

565

Hundreds of years ago, people found that metals made good money. People valued bronze and copper, which could be cut into small pieces just right for carrying around.

To know how much each piece was worth, people just had to weigh it. The heavier the piece of metal, the more it was worth.

These pieces became the first coins.

Then coins were made from silver and gold. People wanted silver and gold, so they were happy to trade for silver and gold coins.

But carrying many coins is difficult, so paper money was **invented**.

The first paper money was like a printed promise, a promise that the money could be taken to a bank and traded for silver and gold coins.

Promissory note

In the United States people no longer use silver and gold coins as money.

But paper money still has value, because you can use it to buy things.

You can use paper money to buy bread, furniture, and clothing. You can use it to buy a house. You can even use paper money to buy silver and gold.

Mexico

Europe

Each country has its own money. In the United States people use dollars. In Mexico people use pesos, in Israel new shekels, in Russia rubles, in China yuan, in Canada dollars, in South Africa rand, and in Brazil reais. People in many of the countries in Europe use euros.

China

Brazil

The value of money in each country keeps changing. One U.S. dollar may be worth ten Mexican pesos one day and a little more or less the next day.

Your dollar may be worth seven Chinese yuan one day and slightly more or less the next day.

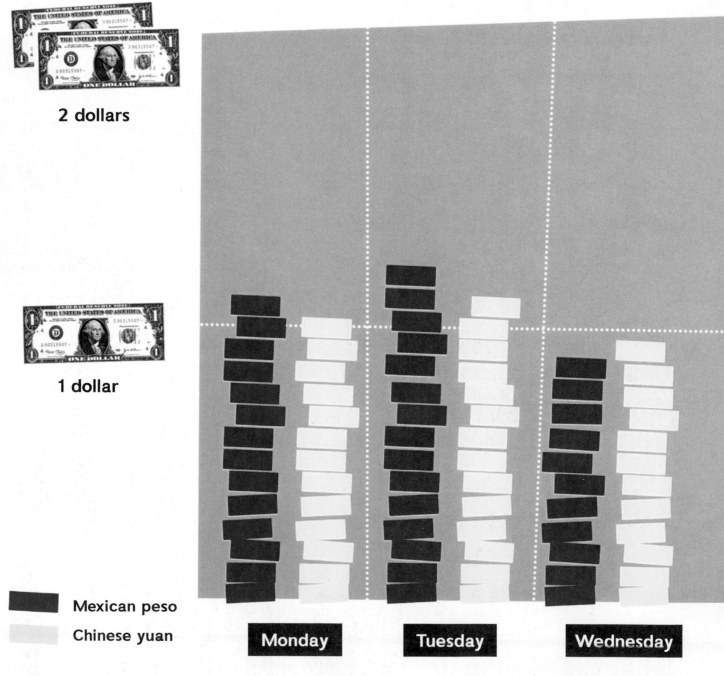

2 dollars

1 dollar

Mexican peso

Chinese yuan

Monday   Tuesday   Wednesday

The value of each country's money goes up when **prices** go down in that country. When that happens, the dollar buys more.

The value of each country's money goes down when prices go up in that country. When prices go up, the same dollar buys less.

6 TOMATOES FOR $1

6 TOMATOES 3 FOR $1

When prices go down, the value of a dollar goes up. For example, when a scoop of ice cream costs one dollar, each dollar buys one scoop. If prices go down and a scoop of ice cream now costs just fifty cents, a dollar buys double what it bought before. Now a dollar buys two scoops of ice cream. The value of a dollar in relation to ice cream went up.

As prices in a country go down, not just for ice cream but for many, even most, things, the value of its currency goes up.

BOOK ORDERS
$15 Abe Lincoln
$15 Mary Cash
$15 Connie Coin
$15 Uncle Sam

COIN Collecting for Beginners

BANK ACCOUNT
Name: Uncle Sam
Funds: $100
Purchase: – $ 15
                    $ 85

COIN Collecting for Beginners
$15
BUY

Checks and credit cards are money too, because they can be used to buy things.

Some people even use digital money. With digital money there is a computer **record** of the money in an account. When you spend that money to buy a book or download music, the amount you spend is subtracted from your account.

Even though you cannot see digital money, it's still money because it can be used to buy things.

STOP AND CHECK

Summarize How does digital money work? Summarize what you have read.

We no longer live in a world with just hunters and food gatherers. We live in a world with dancers, teachers, doctors, astronauts, dentists, and bakers.

Without money, it's hard to imagine what a dancer would trade to buy a car.

Without money, it's hard to imagine what a teacher would trade to buy a sweater.

It's hard to imagine a world without money.

Now reach into your pockets. Do you have any coins? Do you have any paper money? If you do, you're probably pleased.

You know with money you can buy things you want. With money you can buy things you need.

UNCLE SAM'S ALL-AMERICAN ICE CREAM

ABOUT THE AUTHOR AND ILLUSTRATOR

DAVID A. ADLER wrote stories for his younger brothers and sisters when he was growing up. His favorite was one about a girl who planted flowers in her shoes. David says, "I'm still making up stories!" He became an author and has written more than 200 books for children. *Money Madness* is one of several of his books about money and how it works. Some other books David writes are mystery stories and biographies.

EDWARD MILLER always liked to draw pictures as a child. Now he uses a computer to create illustrations for books. His cat Jimmy likes to lie on Edward's arm while he works. Jimmy weighs 14 pounds!

AUTHOR'S PURPOSE

Money Madness has a bar graph on page 568. Why do you think David included this graph in his book? How does it help you understand what David is teaching about money?

Respond to the Text

Summarize

Use important details from the selection to summarize *Life of a Dollar Bill.* Information from your chart may help you.

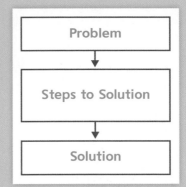

Problem
Steps to Solution
Solution

Write

How does the author help you understand why people use money? Use these sentence starters:

People use money to....
The illustrations and diagrams help me...

Make Connections

Why is a dollar bill important?
ESSENTIAL QUESTION

What can you do with a one-dollar bill?
TEXT TO WORLD

Compare Texts
Read about a king whose wish
for gold causes problems.

KING MIDAS AND THE GOLDEN TOUCH

Many years ago, King Midas lived in a grand palace with a beautiful rose garden. He had one daughter whom he loved very much.

One day, King Midas performed a good deed for a friend, who rewarded King Midas by granting him one wish. King Midas wanted to become rich, but he did not desire **money**. He did not want to **purchase** jewels and goods. Instead, he wanted riches that money could not buy. King Midas wished that everything he touched be turned instantly to gold.

King Midas's friend granted him the wish. King Midas ran over to his garden and touched a rose. The flower instantly turned to gold. King Midas clapped his hands with glee.

Illustration: Anna Vojtech

576

King Midas spent all day turning things to gold. By dinnertime, he was very hungry and thirsty. He sat down to eat with his daughter and his friend. King Midas reached for the food and water on his gold table. But each object he touched turned to gold, leaving him hungry and thirsty.

King Midas's daughter offered him her water. He reached to take it and, without thinking, touched her hand. Immediately, she turned to gold, too! Stunned, King Midas begged his friend, "Undo my wish, please!" Seeing that he had learned his lesson, his friend undid the wish at once. All the golden objects returned to normal, including his daughter.

King Midas hugged his daughter tightly. He had lost his gold, but he had gained back what he truly loved. Some things are worth more than gold.

Make Connections

Instead of using money, what did King Midas use to get rich? ESSENTIAL QUESTION

What are the different forms of money that you have read about this week? TEXT TO TEXT

Essential Question
Where can your imagination take you?
Read how poems express where books can take us.

Go Digital!

Books to the Ceiling

by Arnold Lobel

Books to the ceiling, books to the sky.

My piles of books are a mile high.

How I love them!

How I need them!

I'll have a long beard by the time

I read them.

I've Got This Covered

by Laura Purdie Salas

I'm the first thing you see when you walk by a book.
My picture is shouting, "Please stop! Take a look!"

I've got **dazzling** colors—all you could want.
I wish I had glitter and sparkles to flaunt.

I only have **seconds** to show that you need
to pick up this book, get comfy, and read.

Eating While Reading

by Gary Soto

What is better
Than this book
And the churn of candy
In your mouth,
Or the balloon of bubble gum,
Or the crack of sunflower seeds,
Or a swig of soda,
Or the twist of beef jerky,
Or the slow slither
Of snow cone syrup
Running down your arms?

What is better than
This sweet dance
On the tongue,
And this book
That pulls you in?
It yells, *"Over here!"*
And you hurry along
With a red, sticky face.

Respond to the Text

Summarize

Use important details from "Eating While Reading" to describe the poem's message. Information from your Point of View chart may help you.

Character	Clue	Point of View

Write

How do the poets help you to understand different ways people enjoy reading? Use these sentence starters:

The poet uses...
The poet compares...

Make Connections

Where does reading take you? ESSENTIAL QUESTION

Each poem describes the way reading makes the speaker feel. How does reading make you feel? TEXT TO WORLD

Compare Texts
Read two poems
about creating art.

Clay Play

by Kristine O'Connell George

Pound it, round it,

stretch it, roll it,

braid or bowl it,

mold it, fold it.

Press it flat

and very thin

for daisy petals—

fishes' fin.

Take a lump

(a good-sized chunk)

for oak tree stump

or elephant trunk.

Is it crooked?

Not quite right?

Pound it, round it,

stretch it, roll it,

braid or bowl it.

Fold it, mold it,

until you see

what it *really* wants to be.

Crayons

by Marchette Chute

I've colored a picture with crayons.

I'm not very pleased with the sun.

I'd like it much stronger and brighter.

And more like the actual one.

I've tried with a crayon that's yellow.

I've tried with a crayon that's red.

But none of it looks like the sunlight

I carry around in my head.

Make Connections

? The poems both describe how people **create** art. How do people use their **imagination** to make things? ESSENTIAL QUESTION

"Clay Play" describes how you can use your imagination to make things out of clay. What other ways to use your imagination have you read about this week? TEXT TO TEXT

Glossary

This glossary can help you find the meanings of words in this book that you may not know. The words in the glossary are listed in alphabetical order.

Guide Words

Guide words at the top of each page tell you the first and last words on the page.

anticipation/barbecue

First word on the page

Last word on the page

Sample Entry

Each word is divided into syllables. The way to pronounce the word is given next. You can understand the pronunciation respelling by using the pronunciation key.

Pronunciation

Part of speech

Main Entry & Syllable division

am·bu·lance (am'byə ləns) *noun.*
A special vehicle that is used to carry sick or injured people to a hospital.
My neighbor once called an ambulance to take him to the hospital.

Definition

Example sentence

Pronunciation Key

You can understand the pronunciation respelling by using this **pronunciation key**. A shorter key appears at the bottom of every other page. When a word has more than one syllable, an accent mark (') shows which syllable is stressed.

Phonetic Spelling	Examples
a	**a**t, b**a**d, pl**ai**d, l**au**gh
ā	**a**pe, p**ai**n, d**ay**, br**ea**k
ä	f**a**ther, c**a**lm
âr	c**a**re, p**ai**r, b**ea**r, th**ei**r, wh**ere**
e	**e**nd, p**e**t, s**ai**d, h**ea**ven, fri**e**nd
ē	**e**qual, m**e**, f**ee**t, t**ea**m, p**ie**ce, k**ey**
i	**i**t, b**i**g, g**i**ve, h**y**mn
ī	**i**ce, f**i**ne, l**ie**, m**y**
îr	**ear**, d**eer**, h**ere**, p**ier**ce
o	**o**dd, h**o**t, w**a**tch
ō	**o**ld, **oa**t, t**oe**, l**ow**
ô	c**o**ffee, **a**ll, t**au**ght, l**aw**, f**ou**ght
ôr	**or**der, f**or**k, h**or**se, st**or**y, p**our**
oi	**oi**l, t**oy**
ou	**ou**t, n**ow**, b**ough**
u	**u**p, m**u**d, l**o**ve, d**ou**ble
ū	**u**se, m**u**le, c**ue**, f**eu**d, f**ew**
ü	r**u**le, tr**ue**, f**oo**d, fr**ui**t
ù	p**u**t, w**oo**d, sh**ou**ld, l**oo**k
ûr	b**ur**n, h**ur**ry, t**er**m, b**ir**d, w**or**d, c**ou**rage
ə	**a**bout, tak**e**n, penc**i**l, lem**o**n, circ**u**s
b	**b**at, a**b**ove, jo**b**
ch	**ch**in, su**ch**, ma**tch**
d	**d**ear, so**d**a, ba**d**
f	**f**ive, de**f**end, lea**f**, o**ff**, cou**gh**, ele**ph**ant
g	**g**ame, a**g**o, fo**g**, e**gg**
h	**h**at, a**h**ead
hw	**wh**ite, **wh**ether, **wh**ich
j	**j**oke, en**j**oy, **g**em, pa**g**e, e**dge**
k	**k**ite, ba**k**ery, see**k**, ta**ck**, **c**at
l	**l**id, sai**l**or, fee**l**, ba**ll**, a**ll**ow
m	**m**an, fa**m**ily, drea**m**
n	**n**ot, fi**n**al, pa**n**, **kn**ife, **gn**aw
ng	lo**ng**, si**ng**er
p	**p**ail, re**p**air, soa**p**, ha**pp**y
r	**r**ide, pa**r**ent, wea**r**, mo**r**e, ma**rr**y
s	**s**it, a**s**ide, pet**s**, **c**ent, pa**ss**
sh	**sh**oe, wa**sh**er, fi**sh**, mi**ss**ion, na**ti**on
t	**t**ag, pre**t**end, fa**t**, dress**ed**
th	**th**in, pan**th**er, bo**th**
<u>th</u>	**th**ese, mo**th**er, smoo**th**
v	**v**ery, fa**v**or, wa**v**e
w	**w**et, **w**eather, re**w**ard
y	**y**es, oni**o**n
z	**z**oo, la**z**y, ja**zz**, ro**s**e, dog**s**, house**s**
zh	vi**s**ion, trea**s**ure, sei**z**ure

Aa

a·cross (ə krôs') *adverb*. From one side to the other. *When we got to the bridge, we drove across.*

ac·tions (ak'shəns) *plural noun*. Things someone or something does. *Tim's brave actions made his mother very proud.*

ac·tive (ak'tiv) *adjective*. Lively, busy. *Al is always active and never sits still.*

a·dapt (ə dapt') *verb*. To become used to a place or thing. *Nolan had to adapt to a new school.*

a·dult (ə dult') *noun*. A person who is fully grown. *The adult was in charge of the children.*

ad·ven·ture (ad ven'chər) *noun*. Something exciting that a person does. *Luba went on an adventure in a sailboat.*

a·fraid (ə frād') *adjective*. Feeling fear; scared. *Arthur is afraid of snakes.*

a·gree (ə grē') *verb*. To think the same. *I agree that we should play soccer.*

a·live (ə līv') *adjective*. Having life; living. *You must water the plant to keep it alive.*

al·lowed (ə loud') *verb*. Having permission to do something. *Daneet was not allowed to play video games.*

a·maz·ing (ə māz'ing) *adjective*. Causing great wonder. *The magician did an amazing trick.*

a·mused (ə mūzd') *verb*. Made to smile or laugh. *My family was amused by the funny movie.*

ap·peared (ə pîrd') *verb*. Came into sight. *The sun appeared from behind the cloud.*

a·shamed (ə shāmd') *adjective*. Feeling sorry or upset for doing something wrong or silly. *Pam was ashamed for spilling milk.*

a·side (ə sīd') *adverb*. On or to one side. *Jill put her game aside to do her homework.*

Bb

be·have (bi hāv') *verb*. To act in a certain way. *My parents want me to behave politely.*

be·lieve (bi lēv') *verb*. To think something is true. *I believe the library is close by.*

boast (bōst) *verb.* To brag. *My brother likes to boast about how tall he is.*

bor·row (bär'ō) *verb.* To take and return later. *Kyle had to borrow a pencil from me.*

bur·ied (ber'ēd) *verb.* Covered up or hidden. *The dog buried a bone in the yard.*

Cc

care (kâr) *noun.* Close and kind attention. *Pat takes care of his pet.*

chal·len·ging (chal'ən jing) *verb.* Making someone try hard. *My teacher is always challenging me to do my best.*

cham·pi·on (cham'pē ən) *noun.* Winner. *Our school is the champion in soccer.*

check (chek) *verb.* To see if something is correct. *We check our answers when we are done.*

cheered (chîrd) *verb.* Shouted with happiness. *The crowd cheered when Mia scored.*

choose (chüz) *verb.* To pick something out. *Zina will choose one of the cookies to eat.*

chores (chôrs) *plural noun.* Small jobs. *One of my chores is to make my bed.*

cli·mate (klī'mit) *noun.* The weather in a place over a long time. *The climate in our state is cool and dry.*

com·mon (kom'ən) *adjective.* Belonging to all. *The students use the common area.*

con·cert (kon'sərt) *noun.* A musical program. *Luis saw a concert by his favorite band.*

co·op·er·ate (kō op'ə rāt) *verb.* To work together. *We always cooperate with each other.*

cost (kôst) *noun.* The price of something. *The cost of the toy was five dollars.*

cost·ume (kost'ūm) *noun.* Clothing worn to look like something else. *The actor wore a costume on stage.*

---

at; āpe; fär; câre; end; mē; it; īce; pîerce; hot; ōld; sông; fôrk; oil; out; up; ūse; rüle; pùll; tûrn; chin; sing; shop; thin; **th**is; hw in white; zh in treasure.

The symbol ə stands for the unstressed vowel sound in about, taken, pencil, lemon, and circus.

coun·try·side (kun′trē sīd) *noun.* The land outside of cities and towns. *We drove past farms in the **countryside**.*

cov·ered (kuv′ərd) *verb.* Put over or on top of. *I **covered** the pot with a lid.*

cre·ate (crē āt′) *verb.* To make. *The artist will **create** a painting for us.*

crops (krops) *plural noun.* Plants grown for food. *The farmer planted **crops** in the field.*

cul·ture (kul′chər) *noun.* The way of life for a group of people. *The class is studying the **culture** of the Native Americans.*

cur·i·ous (kyûr′ē əs) *adjective.* Wanting to know about things. *The **curious** kitten explored the house.*

cus·tom·ers (kus′tə mərs) *plural noun.* Buyers at a store or business. *The **customers** at the store buy clothing.*

cus·toms (kus′təms) *plural noun.* A way of acting done by many people. *One of our **customs** is to salute the flag.*

Dd

dam·age (dam′ij) *noun.* Harm that makes something less useful. *The storm caused **damage** to my bike.*

dan·ger·ous (dān′jə rə s) *adjective.* Not safe. *Running with scissors is **dangerous**.*

dash (dash) *verb.* To run in a hurry. *Teach your dog not to **dash** after cars.*

daz·zling (daz′ling) *adjective.* Bright. *The **dazzling** sunlight hurt my eyes.*

de·cide (di sīd′) *verb.* To make up your mind. *Erik had to **decide** which shoes to wear.*

de·li·cious (di li′shəs) *adjective.* Good to taste. *Clare loved eating the **delicious** apple.*

de·light·ed (di līt′id) *adjective.* Greatly pleased. *The crowd was **delighted** by the show.*

de·pend (di pend′) *verb.* To count on someone for help. *I can **depend** on my mom to help me with homework.*

de·scribe (di skrīb′) *verb.* To give a picture of something in words. *My dad asked me to **describe** my day at school.*

de·stroy (di stroi') *verb*. To break apart completely. *An earthquake can destroy a building.*

de·ter·mined (di tûr'mind) *verb*. Decided. *We determined that it was too cold to play.*

de·vel·op (di vel'əp) *verb*. To grow. *Every child will develop into an adult.*

dif·fer·ent (dif'ərənt) *adjective*. Not alike. *My fish is a different color than your fish.*

dis·cov·er (dis kəv'ər) *verb*. To find for the first time. *I want to discover a new park.*

dis·tance (dis'təns) *noun*. A place far away. *From a distance, the mountains looked small.*

dreamed (drēmd) *verb*. Imagined while asleep or awake. *Ty dreamed of flying a plane.*

drops (drops) *plural noun*. Small amounts of liquid. *Sue spilled a few drops of water.*

Ee

ea·ger (ē'gər) *adjective*. Wanting to do something. *The players were eager to start the game.*

Earth (ûrth) *noun*. The planet on which we live. *We need to take care of Earth.*

earth resources (ûrth ri sôr səs) *plural noun*. Useful things that come from the land or water. *Some earth resources give us food.*

edge (ej) *noun*. A line or place where something ends. *The pencil rolled off the edge of the desk.*

eer·ie (îr'ē) *adjective*. Strange and scary. *Ed thought that the eerie house was haunted.*

e·lec·tric·i·ty (i lek tris'i tē) *noun*. A form of energy. *We use electricity to light our home.*

en·er·gy (en'ər jē) *noun*. The ability to do work; power. *Humans get energy from food.*

---

at; āpe; fär; câre; end; mē; it; īce; pîerce; hot; ōld; sông; fôrk; oil; out; up; ūse; rüle; pull; tûrn; chin; sing; shop; thin; this; hw in white; zh in treasure.

The symbol ə stands for the unstressed vowel sound in about, taken, pencil, lemon, and circus.

en·joyed (en joid´) *verb.* Liked very much. *Becky **enjoyed** watching the play.*

e·nor·mous (i nôr´məs) *noun.* Very large. *Dinosaurs were **enormous** creatures.*

en·ter·tained (en tər tānd´) *verb.* Kept interested. *The cat was **entertained** by the ball.*

es·cape (is kāp´) *verb.* To get away. *The baby tried to **escape** from the crib.*

e·vent (i vent´) *noun.* Something that happens. *Winning the game was a happy **event** for us.*

ex·cite (ik sīt´) *verb.* To stir up. *The music will **excite** the crowd.*

ex·cit·ed (ik sīt´id) *adjective.* Feeling very happy and eager. *The **excited** crowd cheered for the singer.*

ex·claimed (ik sklāmd´) *verb.* Said with a strong feeling. *"My bike is missing!" I **exclaimed**.*

ex·plode (ik splōd´) *verb.* To blow up. *The tire will **explode** if you add too much air.*

ex·plo·ra·tion (ik splə rā´shən) *noun.* The act of looking closely. *The divers went on a sea **exploration**.*

ex·press (ik spres´) *verb.* To say or show. *You can **express** your feelings to me.*

Ff

fair (fâr) *adjective.* Equal and just for all sides. *The rules of the game were not **fair**.*

fav·or·ite (fā´vər it) *adjective.* Best-liked. *Summer is my **favorite** time of year.*

feast (fēst) *verb.* To eat very well. *My family will **feast** on turkey.*

feath·ers (feth´ərs) *plural noun.* The soft, light covering of a bird. *The parrot had green **feathers**.*

fi·nal·ly (fī´nə lē) *adverb.* At the end; at last. *We **finally** got home at midnight.*

flap·ping (flap´ing) *verb.* Moving up and down. *The bat was **flapping** its wings to fly.*

flows (flōs) *verb.* Runs like water. *The river **flows** through the village.*

fond (fänd) *adjective.* Enjoying a great deal. *Oscar is **fond** of music.*

force (fôrs) *noun.* Something that moves or stops a body. *The force of the wind blew the tree down.*

form (fôrm) *verb.* To make. *Casey will form a mug out of clay.*

free·dom (frē′də m) *noun.* The ability to move or be free. *The hawks had the freedom to fly.*

fresh (fresh) *adjective.* New; not spoiled. *We picked fresh berries from the bush.*

friend·ship (frend′ship) *noun.* The feeling of being friends. *Our friendship started when we played softball together.*

fur (fər) *noun.* The hair on an animal. *Polar bears have white fur.*

Gg

gent·ly (jent′lē) *adverb.* In a kind or soft way. *She gently picked up the baby.*

gi·ant (jī′ənt) *adjective.* Very large. *The giant truck had large tires.*

glance (glans) *verb.* To look at quickly. *I glance in the mirror before I go to school.*

gold·en (gōl′dən) *adjective.* Having the color or shine of gold. *The golden coin shined in the sun.*

groom (grüm) *verb.* To make clean and neat. *The cat will groom her kittens.*

growth (grōth) *noun.* The act of growing. *The growth of the plant took many weeks.*

grum·bled (grum′bəld) *verb.* Made a low, rumbling sound. *My tummy grumbled when I was hungry.*

Hh

hab·i·tat (hab′i tat) *noun.* The place where an animal lives. *The whale's habitat is the ocean.*

harsh (härsh) *adjective.* Rough or unpleasant. *We stayed in due to the harsh weather.*

---

at; āpe; fär; câre; end; mē; it; īce; pîerce; hot; ōld; sông; fôrk; oil; out; up; ūse; rüle; púll; tûrn; chin; sing; shop; thin; this; hw in white; zh in treasure.

The symbol ə stands for the unstressed vowel sound in about, taken, pencil, lemon, and circus.

haul (hôl) *verb.* To carry something heavy. *The tow truck can* **haul** *the car.*

her·oes (hîr'ōs) *plural noun.* People who are looked up to. *The firemen who saved the family are* **heroes.**

his·to·ry (his'tə rē) *noun.* Events of the past. *The* **history** *of the town goes back many years.*

hol·ler (hol'ər) *verb.* To shout. *Sarah's mom had to* **holler** *her name in the noisy room.*

Ii

i·de·as (ī dē'əs) *plural noun.* Thoughts. *The class had many* **ideas** *for the project.*

i·mag·i·na·tion (i majə nā'shən) *noun.* The ability to create new ideas or images. *Eve used her* **imagination** *to think of a story.*

im·por·tant (im pôr'tənt) *adjective.* Having great meaning. *Eating good food is* **important** *for your health.*

in·sists (in sists') *verb.* To demand. *Sophie* **insists** *that we follow the rules.*

in·stru·ment (in'strə mənt) *noun.* An object that makes music. *Each* **instrument** *makes a different sound.*

in·ter·act (in tər akt') *verb.* To act and react with someone else. *My friend and I* **interact** *at school.*

in·ter·est (in'tər ist) *noun.* A liking for. *The artist had an* **interest** *in painting nature.*

in·vent·ed (in vent'id) *verb.* Created for the first time. *Who* **invented** *the computer?*

in·vit·ed (in vīt'id) *verb.* Asked to come. *Kenny* **invited** *me to his party.*

is·land (ī'lənd) *noun.* Land surrounded by water. *Dad sailed the boat to the* **island.**

is·sues (ish'üs) *plural noun.* Topics that are talked about. *Our parents like to discuss* **issues** *from the news.*

Jj

jobs (jobs) *plural noun.* Work done for pay. *Some people have* **jobs** *in the city.*

jour·ney (jər'nē) *noun.* A long trip. *The* **journey** *took many days to finish.*

Ll

lan·guage (lang'gwij) *noun.* The speech of a group of people. *Jenna knows English and another* **language.**

lay·ers (lā'ərs) *plural noun.* Levels or folds on top of each other. *The cake had three* **layers** *of frosting.*

les·sons (le'səns) *plural noun.* Things to be taught or learned. *Mike took drum* **lessons** *after school.*

live·ly (līv'lē) *adjective.* Full of life or energy. *The playground is a* **lively** *place during recess.*

lo·cal (lō'kəl) *adjective.* In a certain place. *The* **local** *library is near our house.*

lo·ca·tion (lō kā'shən) *noun.* A certain place or position. *What is the* **location** *of your school?*

lone·ly (lōn'lē) *adjective.* Far away from places. *One* **lonely** *house sits in the middle of the desert.*

Mm

ma·chines (mə shēns') *plural noun.* Devices made of parts that do a job. *The* **machines** *in the factory helped make cars.*

mam·mal (ma'məl) *noun.* A type of animal with fur that gives milk. *A dog is a* **mammal.**

mea·sure (me' zhər) *verb.* To find the size of something. *I used a ruler to* **measure** *the room.*

mon·ey (mu'nē) *noun.* Dollars and cents. *She has some* **money** *to buy tickets.*

moon·light (mün'līt) *noun.* The glow from the moon. *The* **moonlight** *shined on the lake.*

move·ments (müv'mənts) *plural noun.* Acts of motion. *The soccer player's* **movements** *got the ball into the goal.*

mu·sic (mü'zik) *noun.* A group of sounds that make songs. *Some* **music** *is loud.*

---

at; āpe; fär; câre; end; mē; it; īce; pîerce; hot; ōld; sông; fôrk; oil; out; up; ūse; rüle; pull; tûrn; chin; sing; shop; thin; this; hw in white; zh in treasure.

The symbol ə stands for the unstressed vowel sound in **about, taken, pencil, lemon,** and **circus.**

Nn

na·ture (nā'chər) *noun.* The part of the world not made by people. *The lake is a part of nature.*

needs (nēds) *plural noun.* Things one must have. *Water is one of a plant's needs.*

neigh·bor (nā'bər) *noun.* Someone who lives nearby. *My neighbor invited me to her house next door.*

ner·vous·ly (nûr'vəs lē) *adverb.* In an uneasy way; not relaxed. *Paola nervously waited for her test score.*

night·time (nīt'tīm) *noun.* The dark part of the day. *We go to bed at nighttime.*

Oo

ob·jects (ob'jekts) *plural noun.* Things. *Interesting objects are on display at the museum.*

off·spring (ôf'spring) *noun.* The young of an animal. *The mother lion had two offspring.*

out·doors (out dôrz') *noun.* Not inside. *We ate outdoors under the tree.*

Pp

pale (pāl) *adjective.* Light in color. *Your shirt looks brighter than my pale one.*

pa·rades (pə rāds') *plural noun.* Marches in honor of something. *Most parades have music.*

pa·tient (pā'shənt) *adjective.* Able to put up with trouble without anger. *The mother was patient with the crying baby.*

peace·ful (pēs'fəl) *adjective.* Calm. *The city is peaceful and quiet in the early morning.*

peeks (pēks) *verb.* Looks quickly. *The shy boy peeks around the corner.*

peered (pîrd) *verb.* Looked closely. *The lost woman peered at her map.*

per·fect·ly (pûr'fikt lē) *adverb.* In an excellent way. *My new shoes fit perfectly.*

per·form (pûr fôrm') *verb.* To do something skillful in public. *The actors will perform in the play.*

plead (plēd) *verb.* To make a request. *We had to beg and plead to stay up late.*

plen·ty (plen′tē) *noun.* Enough of something. *The school has **plenty** of rooms.*

pow·er (pou′ər) *noun.* Energy that can do work. *The toy uses **power** from a battery.*

pre·pare (pri pâr′) *verb.* To get ready. *We **prepare** for a test by studying.*

pre·vent (pri vent′) *verb.* To stop from happening. *Wear a seatbelt to **prevent** getting hurt.*

pri·ces (prī′səs) *plural noun.* The costs. *The **prices** in the store are lower during a sale.*

prom·is·es (präm′is əs) *plural noun.* Statements by people that they say will happen. *My best friend always keeps her **promises**.*

pro·per (prop′ər) *adjective.* Correct. *Lily knows the **proper** way to tie her shoes.*

pro·per·ties (prop′ər tēs) *plural noun.* Qualities of something. *Mei described the **properties** of the rock.*

proud·ly (proud′lē) *adverb.* In a way that shows that one is pleased. *Owen **proudly** held up his trophy.*

proved (prüvd) *verb.* Showed to be true. *Nick **proved** that he could throw far.*

pub·lic (pub′lik) *noun.* All the people of a certain place. *The park is open to the **public**.*

pur·chase (pûr′chəs) *verb.* To buy. *We will **purchase** the new car today.*

Rr

rare·ly (râr′lē) *adverb.* Not often. *Snow **rarely** falls in the spring.*

rec·ord (rek′ərd) *noun.* A report of something that happens. *The teacher keeps a **record** of our grades.*

re·gion (rē′jən) *noun.* A large area. *Each **region** of our country has many cities.*

re·la·tion·ship (rē lā′shən ship) *noun.* A connection between people. *Luiset had a good **relationship** with her dad.*

---

at; āpe; fär; câre; end; mē; it; īce; pîerce; hot; ōld; sông; fôrk; oil; out; up; ūse; rüle; pull; tûrn; chin; sing; shop; thin; this; hw in white; zh in treasure.

The symbol ə stands for the unstressed vowel sound in about, taken, pencil, lemon, and circus.

re·mark·a·ble (rē märk′ə bəl) *adjective.* Not ordinary; wonderful. *You did a **remarkable** job on your poster.*

re·pair (ri pâr′) *verb.* To fix. *The doctor can help **repair** a broken leg.*

res·cue (res′kū) *verb.* To save from danger. *The lifeguard had to **rescue** the swimmer.*

re·spon·si·bil·i·ty (ri spän sə bil′i tē) *noun.* A duty. *It is my **responsibility** to tell the truth.*

rest·less (rest′ləs) *adjective.* Always wanting to move. *The **restless** puppy ran all around the room.*

re·sult (ri zult′) *noun.* Something that happens because of something else. *The mistake was the **result** of carelessness.*

rhy·thm (ri′thəm) *noun.* The repeating of sounds in order. *I hear the **rhythm** of the song.*

rights (rīts) *plural noun.* Claims that cannot be taken away. *One of our **rights** is free speech.*

roam (rōm) *verb.* To wander. *The horses can **roam** in the field.*

rules (rüls) *plural noun.* Guides for how to act. *The game has **rules** to follow.*

rustled (rus′əld) *verb.* Made soft, fluttering sounds. *The leaves **rustled** in the breeze.*

Ss

safe (sāf) *adjective.* Away from harm. *The park is a **safe** place to play.*

sci·en·tif·ic (sī ən tif′ik) *adjective.* Relating to science. *The class did a **scientific** experiment using liquids.*

scur·ries (skûr′ēs) *verb.* Moves quickly. *The mouse **scurries** toward the cheese.*

sea·sons (sē′səns) *plural noun.* One of four parts of the year; spring, summer, fall, winter. *All of the **seasons** have different weather.*

sec·onds (sek′ənds) *plural noun.* Very short periods of time. *Juan only had **seconds** to catch the train.*

se·cret (sē′krit) *noun.* Something hidden or private. *Rahm only told his **secret** to me.*

sense (sens) *noun.* A feeling. *June felt a **sense** of joy when she won.*

shad·ows (shad′ōs) *plural noun.* Dark areas made by blocking light. *We saw our **shadows** on the wall.*

share (shâr) *verb*. To divide and give to others. *Please **share** your books with your sister.*

shin·ing (shī′ning) *verb*. Giving or reflecting light. *The sun was **shining** in the sky.*

si·lence (sī′ləns) *noun*. A lack of sound. *There was **silence** in the house at night.*

si·lent (sī′lənt) *adjective*. Having no sound. *The class reads during **silent** time.*

sim·i·lar·i·ties (sim ə lar′i tēs) *plural noun*. Likenesses. *The two rabbits shared many **similarities** such as brown fur.*

snatch (snach) *verb*. To grab quickly. *The puppy tried to **snatch** the ball from my hand.*

so·lar (sō′lər) *adjective*. Having to do with the sun. *Some homes use **solar** energy.*

sol·id (sol′id) *adjective*. Firm and hard. *The ice was **solid** enough for skating.*

so·lu·tion (sə lü′shən) *noun*. The answer to a problem. *The **solution** to the puzzle was tricky.*

sounds (soundz) *plural noun*. Things that can be heard. *We heard animal **sounds** at the zoo.*

speed (spēd) *noun*. Fast motion. *Tasha's **speed** helped her win the race.*

spend (spend) *verb*. To pay money. *Gail will **spend** her money on a bike.*

spies (spīs) *verb*. Catches sight of. *The bird **spies** a worm in the ground.*

stag·es (stā′jəs) *plural noun*. Steps in a process. *A butterfly goes through **stages** as it grows.*

stares (stârs) *verb*. Looks at for a long time. *The cat **stares** out the window for hours.*

steep (stēp) *adjective*. Having a very sharp slope. *The hill was too **steep** to climb.*

sto·ries (stôr′ēs) *plural noun*. Tales of things that happened. *Our favorite **stories** are about pirates.*

---

at; āpe; fär; câre; end; mē; it; īce; pîerce; hot; ōld; sông; fôrk; oil; out; up; ūse; rüle; pùll; tûrn; chin; sing; shop; thin; this; hw in white; zh in treasure.

The symbol ə stands for the unstressed vowel sound in about, taken, pencil, lemon, and circus.

stud·y (stud′ē) *verb*. To try to learn. *Ethan has to **study** for the test.*

suc·ceed (sək sēd′) *verb*. To do well at something. *To **succeed**, you must practice.*

sup·ply (sə plī′) *noun*. An amount of something that is needed. *Our **supply** of food is almost gone.*

sur·round·ed (sə round′id) *verb*. Shut in on all sides. *The house in the woods was **surrounded** by trees.*

sys·tem (sis′təm) *noun*. An orderly plan. *Our family has a **system** for doing chores.*

Tt

team·work (tēm′wərk) *noun*. The combined effort of a group. *We must use **teamwork** to get the job done.*

tem·per·ate (tem′pər it) *adjective*. Not too hot or cold. *Our state has a **temperate** climate.*

tools (tüls) *plural noun*. Things to work with. *Rose fixed the car with her **tools**.*

trade (trād) *verb*. To give one thing in return for something. *I will **trade** my old car for a new one.*

trav·els (trav′əls) *verb*. Goes somewhere. *Our family **travels** to Mexico every year.*

true (trü) *adjective*. Not false or wrong. *The story about the bears was **true**.*

Uu

un·der·stand (un dər stand′) *verb*. To know or get the meaning of. *I **understand** your question.*

un·der·ground (un dər ground′) *adverb*. Beneath the earth's surface. *Worms live **underground**.*

u·nit·ed (ū nīt′əd) *adjective*. Joined together. *Our **united** town worked together to build a playground.*

Vv

val·ue (val′ū) *noun*. Worth or importance. *The **value** of the house has risen.*

vic·to·ry (vic′tə rē) *noun*. A win. *The team earned its first **victory**.*

vil·lag·es (vil′ij is) *plural noun*. Small groups of houses. *Many **villages** are along the river.*

vol·un·teered (väl ən tird') *verb.* Offered to do something. *Greg volunteered to help.*

votes (vōts) *plural noun.* Choices made in an election. *You need many votes to become president.*

Ww

wan·dered (won'dərd) *verb.* Moved here and there. *I wandered around the store.*

warn·ing (wôr'ning) *noun.* A notice given due to danger. *We heard the warning before the storm.*

weath·er (weth'ər) *noun.* The condition of the air. *The city had bad weather outside.*

weight (wāt) *noun.* How heavy something is. *The weight of the rock made it hard to pick up.*

wild (wīld) *noun.* An area where animals run free. *The lions hunt in the wild.*

wis·dom (wiz'dəm) *noun.* Good judgment in knowing what is right. *My grandpa has wisdom and always knows the right answer.*

won·der (wun'dər) *verb.* To want to know about. *I wonder why the sky is blue.*

worth (wərth) *adjective.* Related to the value. *Do you know how much the necklace was worth?*

writ·ers (rīt'ərs) *plural noun.* People who put their thoughts on paper. *The writers read their stories.*

at; āpe; fär; câre; end; mē; it; īce; pîerce; hot; ōld; sông; fôrk; oil; out; up; ūse; rüle; půll; tûrn; chin; sing; shop; thin; this; hw in white; zh in treasure.

The symbol ə stands for the unstressed vowel sound in about, taken, pencil, lemon, and circus.